PAUL
THE APOSTLE

Hugh Montefiore comes from an Anglo-Jewish family and became a Christian whilst at Rugby School. He was a scholar of St John's College, Oxford, but had his university career interrupted by five years' war service. He trained for the ministry at Westcott House, Cambridge, to which he later returned as Vice-Principal. He was Fellow and Dean of Gonville and Caius College for nine years, and university lecturer in the New Testament. He was vicar of the university church of Great St Mary's from 1963 until 1970, when he was appointed Bishop of Kingston.

He was for many years a member of the Church of England's Doctrine Commission, and is the author of several books, including *Man and Nature* and *A Commentary on the Epistle to the Hebrews*, and has contributed to various Cambridge theological writings, amongst them A. R. Vidler's *Soundings*. His last collection of essays was published under the title *Taking Our Past Into Our Future*.

He was given an Honorary Doctorate by Aberdeen University in 1976 and installed as Bishop of Birmingham in March 1978.

PAUL
THE APOSTLE

HUGH MONTEFIORE

Collins
FOUNT PAPERBACKS

First published in Great Britain by
Fount Paperbacks, London in 1981

© Hugh Montefiore 1981

Made and printed in Great Britain by
William Collins Sons & Co Ltd, Glasgow

To
The Readers of the Church of England

CONTENTS

INTRODUCTION

The origin of this book lay in some Open Lectures I gave years ago when I was a Lecturer in the New Testament at Cambridge University. After adapting this material for a residential course for Readers in 1979, I have since re-written it, adding a couple of chapters.

My hope is that it may be of use to the ordinary reader, and in particular that it may help some of the Church of England's Readers. I have also added annotation, in the hope that the book may also be of use to diploma or degree students who need an introduction to Pauline scholarship.

I have even written a final chapter on what Paul means for today.

Paul holds a special place in my personal affections, partly perhaps because of temperament, partly because I belong to the same race as he did and also came to Christ through a sudden conversion. All 'twice-born' Christians could benefit from remembering that it took Paul many years before he fully matured as a Christian.

HUGH MONTEFIORE

1 PAUL THE MAN

This is a book about Paul. He has never fared very well in popular esteem. Jesus, as he should be, is infinitely popular, even among those who do not accept his divinity. Peter the 'big fisherman'[1] seems a very human figure, a natural leader, but weak and fallible like the rest of us. John is the mystic with his 'spiritual gospel'.[2] But Paul? Perhaps he is a bit intellectual for popular taste. 'He does go on so' is the kind of comment which I have often heard from a layman. He is often thought to have been a puritan, which he was not; and for many people his supposed attitude towards women and marriage is quite enough to condemn him. Reluctant admiration is, I think, a fairly typical response to the Apostle of the Gentiles. Even those who most approve his doctrines do not often venerate him as a man.

Paul has often been sold short. Before going on later to discuss his theology, I want to devote this first chapter to Paul the man, his basic attitudes, his character and characteristics.[3] In order to do this, it is best to go to the source itself. If you want to find out what a painter means by a picture, you can read the critics, but you would be better advised to look at the picture and to see what the painter himself has to say about it. It is the same with Paul. If you want to find out what Paul means by Christianity, or even the kind of person Paul was, do not go to a historian like Luke,[4] but go to the source himself, Paul the Apostle. In any case Luke's Acts are hardly disinterested. He was concerned to show parallels between Paul and Peter.[5] He wanted to depict Christianity as a respectable *religio licita*, and so he shows Paul well treated by the Romans and misunderstood by the Jews.[6] He set out to write the story of how the Good News spread from the capital of Judaea to the capital of the Roman Empire.[7] And so we find Paul depicted as a Pharisee who is misunderstood by Sadducees, a typical Christian convert of his age, who is able to travel around the Roman Empire with the goodwill of the authorities. We hear little about his distinctive teaching – just a small aside about justification by faith in a speech at Pisidian Antioch, which in any case Luke got wrong.[8]

So to Paul's Epistles we turn. But let us start by asking ourselves what we expect to find there. First of all his Epistles are *letters*, which is what the word means. They are not pamphlets or treatises; nor are they, as many students mistakenly seem to regard them, a kind of weekly essay. If we received a missive from a Christian leader, we would not expect to find in it a complete system of dogmatic theology. When we receive a letter, it almost always refers to contemporary happenings or contemporary ideas. Of course it is not quite fair to compare Paul's Epistles with our private letters. Apart from the Pastoral Epistles, all except one of them were written to churches. A better comparison perhaps would be the pastoral letter of a bishop to the churches of his diocese. But this too would deal with matters of belief and order relevant to the situation in the diocese.

And so it is in Paul's Epistles. For example, the two Epistles to the Thessalonians are for the most part concerned with teaching about the Last Day, for Paul's instructions on this matter had been gravely misunderstood. The subject was serious, for some Thessalonian Christians had downed tools, and Paul had to try to put things right. Or again, matters went horribly wrong at Corinth. We often think of scandals in contemporary churches, while the primitive Church, we like to believe, was a model of purity, faith and charity. The two Epistles to the Corinthians soon dispel that illusion. Paul had to deal with matters as shocking as incest, as mundane as clergy stipends, and as apparently trivial as women wearing hats in church. He had to cope with the theological issues of unity – for the Corinthians had already begun the deplorable Christian habit of dividing the Church into sects. He had to deal with the Holy Communion, which had not yet been separated from a fellowship meal, and some Christians had made pigs of themselves before their fellow Christians had even arrived! He had to deal with questions of resurrection – for some at Corinth believed that there was no resurrection from the dead. Incidentally these matters have a curiously modern ring. We have been reminded of 'the peril of modernizing Jesus'[9] and we must equally beware of the peril of modernizing Paul. None the less there are some matters of Christian belief which are perennial sources of friction down the centuries. Similarly, when we come to consider Paul's attitudes and character, there are some personal characteristics of Paul which speak to us today in contemporary terms despite a vast difference in cultural outlook.

The pastoral matters with which Paul had to cope in his correspondence often bring out his profoundest theology. (Once again, it is the same today. When theology is divorced from pastoral practice, it becomes airborne and irrelevant.) For example, it is while dealing with the question of church collections that Paul gives us a brilliant insight into the nature and mission of Christ – 'For you know how generous our Lord Jesus Christ has been: he was rich, yet for your sakes he became poor, so that through his poverty you might become rich' (2 Corinthians 8:9).[10] Paul often had to combat what he regarded as false and pernicious teaching. But it was often this false teaching that coloured and controlled Paul's definition of the most profound mysteries. For instance, in Colossae Christians had been much influenced by some contemporary and 'progressive' Jewish teaching which had absorbed Hellenistic ways of thinking – we are,

I think, all familiar with the way in which modern ideas can distort religious truth. The Christians in Colossae spoke of the *pleroma*, the fullness, by which they understood the totality of the divine attributes; and they allowed Jesus to contribute a share of these. Paul decided to reply to them in their own language. God, he said, is the *pleroma*; but Christ is not just a part of it. No, in Christ dwelt all the *pleroma* in a bodily way (Colossians 2:9) – as good a description of the Incarnation as anyone could wish for. If we are fully to understand Paul's thoughts, we must look at these particular situations out of which he spoke. He often played an away match on his opponents' ground, using their terminology, but transforming and baptizing it.

This is the kind of way in which Paul's mind worked. Some people work from a set of principles, and apply them rigidly to each and every situation. Paul did not have a mind that worked like that. He reacted existentially. In a given situation he responded in a particular kind of way; in a different situation he would have reacted quite differently. Paul had insight, and a leaping, darting mind. His intellect was pugnacious, and it functioned intuitively. Paul was aggressive by nature, and you will find, if you read his Epistles carefully, that the argument proceeds by contrasts. Here lies the clue to his thought. Some people function by building up a huge intellectual skyscraper. I recollect taking, many years ago, some students from a theological college to St Catherine's, Windsor Great Park, to meet the great theologian Paul Tillich. I remember how he responded to a student's question by going back to first principles, and building up a huge architectonic superstructure until finally he reached the point about which he was asked. One floor of the building was built upon another until finally the conclusion was reached. That was Paul Tillich. Not so Paul of Tarsus. His mind worked by contrasting one point against another, a third against a fourth, by a kind of theological dialectic. This method provides us with brilliant epigrams, memorable aphorisms, incisive battle thrusts. It does not give us a systematic theology.

We might expect Paul to think in a tough kind of way, because he was a tough kind of person. 'A sturdy little baldheaded man, with meeting eyebrows and a rather prominent nose.' That is the earliest description of Paul, written about a hundred years after his death; and the description continues: 'full of grace, for sometimes he appeared like a man, and sometimes he had the face of an angel.'[11] Whether or not it is based on fact, it is the kind of description we might have expected. Paul was clearly insignificant to look at. His enemies used this as a smear, and Paul knew that there was something in it, and he didn't like it (2 Corinthians 10:10). Incidentally they also said that 'as a speaker he is beneath contempt' – an accusation which should surely put fresh heart into all those who feel inadequate as they struggle to preach adequately the Word of God. But despite appearances Paul was tough. It is true that from time to time he alludes to illness, and there have been many speculations about this – malaria, epilepsy, failing eyesight, depression, among others; but the fact is that we simply do not know what his malady was. The New English Bible, for example, lists as alternative renderings 'a sharp physical pain' and 'a painful wound to my pride', which shows the ambiguity of the Greek text at this point (2 Corinthians 12:7). Elsewhere he speaks of despairing of life (2 Corinthians 1:8). But he survived. He tells us that in addition to Roman scourgings, he had been beaten by the Jews no less than five times. Thirty-nine strokes was the maximum they were allowed, and the punishment was much worse than a cat-o'-nine-tails. On another occasion he was stoned (incidentally the Jewish method of execution) and nearly killed. He was shipwrecked on no less than four occasions during one of which he suffered twenty-four hours' exposure in the open sea (2

Corinthians 11:25). These do not suggest that he was a valetudinarian or a hypochondriac! He could take any amount of battering, intellectual or physical. He speaks of himself as 'demolishing sophistries and all that rears its proud head against the knowledge of God. We compel every human thought to surrender in obedience to Christ; and we are prepared to punish all rebellion when once you have put yourselves in our hands' (2 Corinthians 10:5f). There could be 'trouble at every turn, quarrels all round us, fears within' (2 Corinthians 7:5); but nothing could keep this little man permanently down.

Paul tells us very little about his background in his existing letters, except that he was a Jew of the tribe of Benjamin (Romans 11:1). He was proud enough to mention this fact, for it showed his social status. The Benjamites used to own the rich lowlands, and their social standing was high in New Testament times,[12] when people still remembered their tribes in the same kind of way as Highlanders still remember their clans, although they seldom nowadays denote their domicile. The Acts of the Apostles inform us that Paul studied under Rabbi Gamaliel, a famous Jewish guru.[13] Had he been brought up in Jerusalem, or had he gone there from the Diaspora as a student? We do not know. Again the Acts inform us that his home town was Tarsus, and if we accept this – and there is no reason to doubt it – we do not know how long his parents had settled there. He had a married sister, and his nephew saved him from an ambush planned to kill him between Jerusalem and Caesarea (Acts 23:12ff). Jewish boys were expected to marry young and to procreate a son before they were nineteen, but Paul gives no indication that he had ever been married in the past. He certainly was a single man by the time he wrote 1 Corinthians (1 Corinthians 7:7).

Clearly Paul comes from an urban background. Jesus speaks of corn growing, the harvest, the vineyards and the grass of the field. These are his natural images. They are not those of Paul. 'Does God care for cattle?' he asked, as though such a thing could hardly be conceived – a question asked, strangely enough, in connection with his expenses as an Apostle (1 Corinthians 9:9)! On only one occasion, in his existing Epistles, does Paul risk a botanical metaphor, and it is clear from this that Paul never had and never could graft a wild olive (Romans 11:17)! The images with which Paul is most at home are quite different; the army – 'I have fought the good fight'; the race course – 'I have run the race'; the ringside – 'I am like a boxer that does not beat the air'; the market – 'You are bought with a price'. These may be the metaphors of a rhetorician: they are also the images of a townsman.

The Acts of the Apostles tell us that Paul was a Roman citizen; and, again, there is no reason to doubt this information. Although this is not directly confirmed in the Epistles, there is something of an imperial strategy about Paul.[14] It may be that when travelling in the Roman Empire he preferred to be called by the Roman name Paul rather than Saul. At all events he is so called in Acts 13:13 on his first missionary journey. He uses the Roman roads; he spends three years in Ephesus, the 'second city' of the Roman Empire (Acts 20:31); and he finally brings the Good News to its capital city. His letter to the Romans is the longest of his extant Epistles, and it is the place where we find the most careful and systematic exposition of Christianity as he understands it. Roman citizenship would have added to his social standing, rather like a royal birthday honour bestowed on some worthy Member of the British Empire.

Before his conversion Paul was a Rabbi. This is clear from his rabbinical theologizing, and particularly from his method of exposition of the Old Testament scriptures. There are some who see in Rabbinism the key to all his thinking.[15] It was a point of honour that Rabbis pursue a manual trade, lest they should make money out of their piety. Paul had a trade, he made tents. As Professor Dodd has remarked, a man born to manual labour does not speak selfconsciously of 'wearing ourselves out working with our own hands'[16] (I Corinthians 4:12). The whole passage repays study.

> We are weak: you are so powerful. We are in disgrace: you are honoured. To this day we go hungry and thirsty and in rags; we are roughly handled; we wander from place to place: we wear ourselves out working with our own hands.

These are the words of one who is used to respect, and who finds it hard to be treated like a dropout, and to engage in physical overtime.

Paul then was a well-to-do Jewish bourgeois; a Roman citizen who was at home in the Roman world, and a Jew. He came from a Hellenistic city. Tarsus was a provincial university town.[17] Whether Paul studied at the university we do not know, but he was certainly aware of the currents of Greek thought. His letters show a knowledge of the rudiments of Stoic thought and an acquaintance with the Gnostic speculations of his time.[18] He would have known well the Greek Bible, and he would have been well acquainted with pagan religious rites, for he would have met them at every street corner. Indeed there are those who see the clue to his thinking in the Hellenistic thought of his day. Whether or not this is so, it is certain that light can be shed on his thinking by a study of the surviving inscriptions and papyri of the Hellenistic world.[19] For example, he speaks of the Spirit as the 'pledge of what is to come'. The word translated pledge was used in his day to denote the first instalment on a hire purchase. Or again, Paul often uses the imagery of freedom, redemption, in connection with the death of Christ. It is likely that this imagery is taken from the pagan world, where manumission of slaves was achieved by the payment of a sum, and the fiction that the slave, on achieving freedom, became the slave of a god.[20] The imagery is used by Paul to describe the freedom from sin achieved for the Christian through the death of Christ.

Paul was a Hellenistic Jew. There were more Jews outside Judaea than inside it; at least four million in the Diaspora[21] and about half a million inside Judaea.[22] The Jews in the Dispersion had to tread warily. Antisemitism was rife in New Testament times. We know of an appalling putsch in Alexandria, and of the banishment of Jews from Rome. Jews were marked out from Gentiles in the Dispersion by their own stringent rules of food and of morality. They were often rich, always odd, and they formed a minority. No wonder they were unpopular. And Paul was intensely aware of being a Jew, a member of the Chosen People. His Jewish pride never left him, even after his conversion: 'circumcised on my eighth day, Israelite by race, of the tribe of Benjamin, a Hebrew born and bred' (Philippians 3:5). He points out more than once that his Jewish credentials are better than those of his Jewish opponents. 'Are they Hebrews? So am I. Israelites? So am I. Abraham's descendants? So am I . . . I can outdo them' (2 Corinthians 11:22). Paul preached to the Gentiles, and yet even to the end of his days the fact that God called both Jews and Gentiles remained for him a mystery, that is to say, a revealed secret, still something to marvel over.

If Paul gloried in being a Jew, how much must he have gloried in the Jewish law! For the law was God's special gift to his chosen people. Paul could never bring himself to say, even after he had rejected the law as a way to God, that it was evil in itself. In the Epistle to the Romans, where he has harder things to say about the Jewish law than anywhere else, he must still needs write: 'The law is in itself holy, and the commandment is holy and just and good.'

What was this Jewish law? It was a comprehensive

code of living. It contained instruction, teaching, history and worship. It had to be brought up to date. Paul was a Pharisee born and bred. It was the boast of Pharisees that they brought the law up to date, and made it relevant to ordinary life. In fact they made it so relevant that almost every detail of living seemed to be regulated by it. The application of the law to life was known as *Halachah*, and it was a constantly evolving tradition. But the basic commandments were in the law.

This law, or Torah, as its Hebrew name is called, Paul had loved to obey. He even wrote of himself before his conversion: 'In legal rectitude, faultless' (Philippians 3:6). This was a proud boast: it shows us something of the energy and willpower of the man. And yet it left him hopeless and dejected. The more he fulfilled the law, the more he felt that he had failed it. We can give several reasons for this paradoxical state of affairs. First comes the psychological principle. 'I should never have known what it was to covet, if the law had not said "Thou shalt not covet"' (Romans 7:7–8). The principle of contra-suggestion is well known in our day, so that a mother is well advised not to leave the house with the words to her child 'Don't turn on the gas, darling', or she may find the house burnt down on her return! We all know the way in which we find that a veto arouses in us the desire to break it. And, secondly, Paul knew that if he kept the law, he had to keep every jot and tittle of the law; for he quotes the saying from the law: 'Cursed are all those who do not persevere in doing everything that is written in the Book of the Law' (Galatians 3:10). One of the all but inevitable effects of keeping all the commandments of a written code is that a person who does this has a feeling of strong self-satisfaction at his own achievement. But if he has this strong feeling of satisfaction at his achievement (or his 'works' as Paul puts it) then he has offended against the spirit of the law, for its chief commandment is 'Thou shalt love the Lord thy God with all thy soul and strength'. We are ordered to put our trust not in ourselves but in God. It therefore follows that a man who keeps all the injunctions of the law still fails to keep the whole law.

Paul had a boundless desire to excel. The principle of comprehensive schooling would, I think, have made little appeal to him: he always wanted to get to the top. 'In the practice of our national religion I was outstripping many of my contemporaries in my boundless devotion to the traditions of my ancestors', he writes about himself (Galatians 1:14). Already we can imagine the mounting tension of the growing conflict within himself. The harder he tried, the more he failed. The more he failed, the harder he tried. It was a vicious circle, forcing him to spin faster and faster in order to keep up with himself.

It is well known that when a person wants to take it out on himself, he can often relieve his guilt feelings to a certain extent by taking it out on other people instead. We can externalize a conflict that rages within ourselves. Paul tried that. There was a new sect of Jews, followers of a man whom they believed to have been Messiah, the Anointed Jewish Leader who was expected. These men, it seems, were not yet called Christians: they were known as Nazarenes. They claimed just those very things that Paul wanted for himself – or rather the things that one part of him wanted, but which the dominant part had managed to suppress. 'How savagely I persecuted the Church of God and tried to destroy it', he writes (Galatians 1:13). 'I had persecuted the Church of God, and am therefore inferior to all other apostles – indeed, not fit to be called an apostle' he told the Corinthians. We may note that Paul always cast himself in superlative terms: if he could not think of himself as a great saint, at least he would speak of himself as a great sinner!

And then it happened. The Acts of the Apostles give

us no less than three accounts of what it was that took place on the road to Damascus (Acts 9:1–22; 22:3–16; 26:9–18). Paul himself, in his autobiographical passages, speaks more modestly. 'In his good pleasure God, who had set me apart from birth and called me through his grace, chose to reveal his son to me' (Galatians 1:15) he told the Galatians. To the Corinthians he wrote simply: 'In the end he appeared even to me' (1 Corinthians 15:8). In the end reality could no longer be suppressed. As someone who has also been brought up in the Jewish faith, and who has been converted in a not altogether dissimilar experience (although in a lesser mode and in less dramatic circumstances), I do not think that there is much to be gained by considering the details of Paul's conversion. Genuine transcendental experiences are, strictly speaking, incommunicable. They carry their own authenticity. They are necessarily clothed in the language and imagery of the time for reasons of intelligibility. It is interesting that, although minor details of the three accounts of Acts are different, the main points are similar. I do not think that we can doubt the authenticity of the words which formed themselves in Paul's self-consciousness: It is hard for you to kick against the pricks.' But it is easy to fail to see the significance of other words in this spiritual experience: 'Saul, Saul, why do you persecute me?' Paul was not persecuting Jesus, he was persecuting the Church. And yet the voice said 'I am Jesus whom you are persecuting.' In other words, right back at that initiatory experience Paul had identified Jesus with the Church, or at least he had realized that in persecuting the Church he was persecuting Jesus.

It is often the case that only after something is behind us can we recognize it for what it is. When we are immersed in it, our sight seems ill focused. That was the case with Paul. Looking back on that fierce, exacting, puritanical life that he had lived, straining every nerve to be the best Jew, the best Pharisee, the best Rabbi that there had ever been, Paul now sees its hollowness. But he could not see it earlier. When we look at Paul's extant writings describing his basic convictions after his conversion, we find that two predominate – one positive, one negative. The positive conviction is that the living Christ is the answer to all existence; the answer to personal problems, the answer to national, corporate, even cosmic problems – for Paul, to live is Christ. That is the positive aspect. And the negative conviction is that the law is a hindrance rather than a help, and that those who are living by the law are making a hell for themselves. It was not until he was freed from the law that he was able to realize what a dreadful burden it had been for him.

It seems that right from the start Paul came to know that he had been set apart by God to take the Gospel to the Gentiles. In the Acts of the Apostles it is actually Peter who is the first to welcome a Gentile convert (Acts 10). Paul, however, speaking of his conversion, writes to the Galatians that God 'chose to reveal his Son to me and through me, in order that I might proclaim him to the Gentiles' (Galatians 1:16). It seems then as though this calling came to him from the first moment that he became a Christian. Why was Paul such an active missionary, so tireless in spreading the Good News of Christ around the Mediterranean world? It was partly because if Christ really was the truth, it would have been selfish to keep this Good News to himself. It was partly because God had called him to be an evangelist. Partly perhaps it was for a rather different reason. There are those who believe that Paul was a universalist, keen to bring the Good News to all the world.[23] But there is another explanation possible. Paul cared most deeply about his own fellow Jews. His 'deepest desire and prayer is for their salvation' (Romans 10:2). He is a missionary to the Gentiles, and as such he gives all honour to that ministry when he tries to stir emulation in

23

the men of *his own* race 'and so to save some of them' (Romans 11:14). All Israel cannot be saved until the Gentiles have been admitted to the Church in full strength (Romans 11:25). Paradoxically enough, the main reason for his missionary activity among Gentiles could be precisely his deeply felt yearning that his fellow Jews can then be saved.[24]

It seems clear that Paul temperamentally rather liked being 'odd man out' among the apostles. He did not go to Jerusalem until three years after his conversion, and then he only stayed for a fortnight (Galatians 1:18). Paul swears before God that on that visit he saw only Peter and James the Lord's brother. It was when he went up fourteen years later that he met the rest of them. He writes of them somewhat ambiguously. They are 'men of high reputation (not that their importance matters to me: God does not recognize these personal distinctions)' – clearly there are deep emotions running here (Galatians 2:6). They seem to be focused on the emotive subject of circumcision. It was fundamental to Paul's Gospel that a man should be put into a right relationship with God through Christ *by faith alone*, and so circumcision could not be regarded as necessary for salvation for a Gentile convert. Paul seems strangely ambiguous about what happened when the Greek Titus accompanied him to Jerusalem. Perhaps he is embarrassed, perhaps he is merely so distressed at the suggestion of circumcision that he is not his usual coherent self. He does not spare his language on this or other occasions about the Circumcision Party. Here he calls them 'sham Christians, interlopers' (Galatians 2:4). Later, in the Epistle to the Philippians, he describes them as dogs, and even goes on to use really coarse and offensive language – 'The Snippers' (Philippians 3:2). He felt almost as strongly about those who disrupted table fellowship between Jewish and Gentile Christians. True to his conviction that the men of reputation were of little importance to him, he withstood Peter to the face at Antioch, 'because he was clearly in the wrong' (Galatians 2:11). None the less he really did desire a reconciliation between the Jewish and Hellenistic branches of the Church, and he set his heart on a great collection for the mother church at Jerusalem. It was a kind of concrete token of his concern for the unity of Christendom. He introduces it tactfully into his extant correspondence, and he is careful to see that it is brought to the capital by representative members of different churches.[25] It was almost a kind of Christian equivalent to the Jewish temple tax,[26] and it was evidently close to his heart. But he did not favour Gentile Christians in themselves (Romans 2:11). He simply insisted that in Christ there is neither Jew nor Gentile, 'He is himself our peace. Jews and Gentiles, he has made the two one' (Ephesians 2:14). Here we find the clue to Paul's very practical approach to Christian behaviour. 'I am all things to all men', he writes (1 Corinthians 9:22), but he goes on to add 'so that I may by some means save some'. Was Paul a trimmer? Does he really belong to that doubtful tradition in Christian ethics which affirms that the means always justify the ends? By no means! Paul respected Jewish susceptibilities over observance of the Jewish law, so long as these were not imposed on Gentiles. And there is nothing wrong in eating non-Kosher meat in a heathen temple, but if this practice is going to ruin the faith of a 'weak' brother Christian, then it *is* wrong (1 Corinthians 8:7–13). In another letter he amplifies this teaching. 'Those of us who have a robust conscience must accept as our own burden the tender scruples of weaker men, and not consider ourselves' (Romans 15:1). Christians must pursue the things that make for peace and build up the common life (Romans 14:19).

None the less, the very strong and abusive language that he used about his Jewish opponents who attempted to impose the Jewish law on Gentile converts is bound to raise the question of how deep Paul's conversion really went. It is not an easy question to answer. Certainly Paul's allegiance was wholly to Christ. The question is rather to what extent he showed from the time of his conversion a deep Christlikeness in his attitudes and behaviour. It is a common observation about the newly converted that it often takes some time before the Divine Compassion which has taken hold of them really transforms them in the depth of their being and in those deep places of the heart where basic attitudes are formed. Indeed we would hardly expect old traits to disappear overnight. He certainly gave a distorted view of Rabbinic Judaism, although he was unaware of doing this. Undoubtedly Paul remained a somewhat prickly personality. The author of Acts, who is usually inclined to play down differences between his *dramatis personae*, records that Paul had such a row with Barnabas and John Mark that they had to part company, the latter two going back to Cyprus and Paul going on with Silas through Syria and Cilicia (Acts 15:36ff).

Paul shows particular sensitivity over the question of money. 'The Lord gave instructions that those who preach the Gospel should earn their living by the Gospel. But I have never taken advantage of any such right, nor do I intend to claim it in this letter', he writes to the Corinthians (1 Corinthians 9:14). Professor Dodd points out how he tries to conceal his embarrassment at having to take money by the form of words which he uses to the Philippians, using technical terms of trade, as if to give the transaction a severely business aspect.[27] This was a man who had chosen poverty as his lot for ideal ends, but could never feel himself one of the 'poor' to whom alms might be given without suspicion of offence (Philippians 4:15–19). One must admit that there is still a certain egoism in Paul's temperament, even after his conversion. For example, he uses the word 'boast', in

one or other of its compounds, a very great deal – fifty
times altogether, compared with four other instances in
the whole of the New Testament! It is one of his
favourite words. True, once he used to boast of his own
works, and now he uses it to boast of Christ; but the
point is that, unselfconsciously indeed, he still boasts!
And he is somewhat sensitive about his missionary area.
He is absolutely sincere in his desire that his converts
shall not place loyalty to Paul above loyalty to Christ,
but he is obviously not ready to tolerate easily their
feeling a superior loyalty to any other human being.
'Though you have countless guides in Christ', he writes
to the Corinthians, 'you do not have many fathers. For I
became your father in Christ Jesus through the Gospel'
(1 Corinthians 4:15). He is meticulous about his own
sphere of interest and will not trespass beyond it (2
Corinthians 10:12–18). When he writes 'I laid the
foundation and another man is building upon it' the
clear impression is given that the 'other man' is not
wholly welcome to him (1 Corinthians 3:10). The people
to whom he wrote were '*my* people' just as what he
preached was '*my* Gospel'. Not that he ever pretended
that he was perfect (Philippians 3:12). 'Who is weak and
I am not weak?' he asks (2 Corinthians 11:29).

Of course we can easily make too much of all this. The
man who composed the great and unsurpassed Hymn of
Love in 1 Corinthians 13 (and there is no good reason to
suppose that he did not write it himself) knew Christian
love from the inside. Again and again in his Epistles we
have warm injunctions to Christian love. Even if in the
early Thessalonian correspondence he threatened
flaming fire from heaven for all who could not accept
Christ (2 Thessalonians 1:6–8), in the same correspondence he also wrote 'See to it that no one pays back
wrong for wrong but always aim at doing the best you
can for one another and for all men' (1 Thessalonians
5:15). In particular the personal letter to Philemon gives

a touching insight into his personal relationships with friends. Paul had enemies but also many such friends. His strongly emotional nature was capable of much tender love and affection. He could be courteous and tactful, charming and grateful; and he knew that praise and gratitude were more effective than chiding and exhortation in bringing out the best in his congregations. He had on his hands 'the care of all the churches' (2 Corinthians 11:28) and no doubt there were times when the pressure told. If he could be moody and prone to indignation he could also be practical and sensible and quick to reconcile. (For example, he was more gifted in ecstatic utterance than any, but he insists that 'tongues' are for private use (1 Corinthians 14:13–33).) His volatile emotional life meant that he was open to the promptings of God in his heart. Indeed he speaks in mystical terms of his relationship with him.

I know a Christian man who fourteen years ago (whether in the body or out of it, I do not know – God knows) was caught up as far as the third heaven. And I know that this same man (whether in the body or out of it, I do not know – God knows) was caught up into Paradise and heard words so secret that human lips may not repeat them (2 Corinthians 12:2–4).

Paul was obviously speaking about himself. He was a person of real, deep religious experience. Even for Paul, religion went deeper than theology.[28] To understand the man we must look here for the key to his personality. He sees all things in Christ. This mystical experience has been thought by some to be at the heart of the Pauline gospel.[29] Nor can we attribute such mysticism to one occasion only. 'In Christ' is one of his favourite expressions, and often its context shows that it is not used merely in a reductionist sense.

None the less the old traits still remained. No doubt

the old roughnesses were gradually eroded through the love of Christ. However there occurred to him at Corinth an experience which Professor Dodd has likened to a 'second conversion'.[30]

Corinth was the most difficult of all his spiritual children. Already when 1 Corinthians was written, there were troubles enough. That letter did not settle them. Paul decided to pay a quick visit from Ephesus (where he was living) in order to settle them. He failed disastrously. He was outvoted, outmanoeuvred, outspoken by his adversaries. It was a crisis of authority, and Paul had lost it. He returned to Ephesus smarting under this terrible humiliation. He wrote to the Corinthians a letter full of distress, resentment and humiliation. We find this letter in 2 Corinthians 10–13. If we compare this letter with the first part of that Epistle (2 Corinthians 1–9), we find an utterly different attitude. The first part of the Epistle is really a different letter, written after the second half had been sent.[31]

In the intervening period it appears that Paul was ill, even that he thought he would die (2 Corinthians 1:8). We can almost see him fighting his humiliation. And out of this personal crisis came something akin to a second conversion; an interior change of attitude which embodied not resentment but acceptance.

Three times I begged the Lord to rid me of it, but his answer was: 'My grace is all you need: power comes to its full strength in weakness.' I shall therefore prefer to find my joy and pride in the very things that are my weakness; and then the power of Christ will come and rest upon me. Hence I am well content, for Christ's sake, with weakness, contempt, persecution, hardship and frustration; for when I am weak, then I am strong (2 Corinthians 12:8–10).

Paul had written much about the death and resurrection

of Christ before this; even of dying and rising with Christ. Now he had experienced something of this in his own soul. He found himself able to accept himself fully as he really was. And by so doing he found a new release and a new freedom. He was able to live out on a deeper level his profound belief in justification through faith,[32] for he could abandon himself to God's providence without reserve and without fear. We find this attitude prevalent not only in the first half of 2 Corinthians, but also in the so-called Captivity Epistles to the Colossians, Philippians and Ephesians. Here Paul freely admits his limitations. 'I do not reckon myself already to have attained', he writes to the Philippians. 'All I can say is this: forgetting what is behind, and reaching out for what is in front, I press towards the goal to win the prize . . .' And he continues, 'Let us then keep to this way of thinking, those of us who are mature. If there is any point on which you think differently, God will make it clear to you. Only let our conduct be consistent with the level which we have already attained' (Philippians 3:12–16). In his new found Christian maturity, Paul no longer frets about weaknesses, failures and frustrations: he no longer glories in the sufferings which he has to undergo. He writes in the fullness of Christian maturity: 'I have learned to find resources in myself whatever my circumstances. I know what it is to be brought low, and I know what it is to have plenty. I have been very thoroughly initiated into the human lot with all its ups and downs; fullness and hunger, plenty and want. I have strength for anything through him who gives me power!' (Philippians 4:11–13).

What a world of difference from the Paul who was first converted! When once he was world-denying now he is world-affirming. As he changes his attitudes, so also we note a change in his theology. We may well ask how it could be that someone who had been a Christian for so many years would change his basic attitude to the world, and some of his theological views, later in his life. The answer, I think, lies in the nature of the very acute spiritual crisis which he underwent at the hands of the Corinthians, and the new and more deeply Christian attitudes that emerged as a result.

In the early days of his conversion Paul believed that the world would shortly come to an end, and he shared this belief with many of his fellow Christians and fellow Jews. So strongly did he speak that many Thessalonians understood him to mean that the Day of the Lord had already come (2 Thessalonians 2:2)! By the time that he wrote 1 Corinthians, the perspective had lengthened, for he wrote that not all would be dead, some would still be alive on that day (1 Corinthians 15:51). By the time that he wrote to the Romans he simply expressed himself by saying 'Now is our salvation nearer than when we believed' (Romans 13:11). By the time of the Captivity Epistles, he merely writes that Christians are expecting a Saviour from heaven, without any indication of time whatever (Philippians 3:20).

When Paul believed that the world order was in immediate danger of being ended, we can hardly expect him to have taken a very positive view of the things of this world. And so it was. In his earlier letters Paul does not run down marriage, because his Master spoke of it in positive terms, and he saw it as a remedy against fornication for those who had not the gift of continence. He admits it as a relief: he cannot commend it as an ideal (1 Corinthians 7:6). But by the time that the Epistle to the Ephesians has been written, the attitude is quite different. Marriage is actually used as an analogy of the permanent relationship between Christ and his Church – the institution of marriage could hardly be spoken of in higher terms. It is not only his attitude to marriage that is changed. Political institutions are thought of in much more positive terms. Once he had thought that it was a scandal to use secular courts to settle Christian disputes

(1 Corinthians 6:1–4), but by the time of the Epistle to the Romans he has come to regard Roman magistrates as servants of God – the Greek word could almost be translated 'priests of God'. Earlier he had tried to persuade Christians to keep out of the world. In a fragment (2 Corinthians 6:14–7:15) he had written: 'Can light consort with darkness? Can Christ agree with Belial? Or a believer join hands with an unbeliever?' How removed this is from the acknowledgement in the Epistle to the Romans of the instinctive goodness of the natural man: 'When pagans who do not possess the law carry out its precepts by the light of nature, then although they have no law, they are their own law, for they display the effect of the law inscribed on their hearts' (Romans 2:14f). He had come to accept the world as having a positive value which could be transformed in Christ.

It is instructive to see the growing maturity of this giant among Christians. Although he says very little about Jesus in the days of his flesh, and only occasionally quotes from his sayings, we can note a growing Christlikeness in his inner attitude and deepest feelings. It is only human to grow. It is not a criticism of Paul that he took a lifetime to mature in stature as a Christian. None of us can command what happens in the unconscious parts of our personalities: if we could, they would cease to be unconscious. What we have been affects what we shall be. Human beings are motivated by the future, but they cannot abandon their past; and God does not alter our characters, he redirects them so that they can be used as he intends them to be used. It is only when we have accepted ourselves as we are, that we are free to see adversity not as the buffetings of Satan but as the opportunity God gives us for future growth.

I have tried in this opening chapter to give a sketch, so far as the evidence allows us to do so, of Paul the man. He was a remarkable man on any showing. He had a genius for religion, unflagging devotion, a razor-sharp mind and a very large heart. His will was inflexible. A man with such talents would have made his mark in any age and in any occupation. God chose him at the start of the Christian era as his Apostle to the Gentiles, and without him, who can know whether there would be any Christianity at all today?

2 PAUL THE APOSTLE

An apostle is one who is sent. That is what the word means. In Jewish legal thought, a *shaliach* (the Hebrew word which means *apostolos*) has full power of attorney. According to the frequently quoted Rabbinic maxim, 'The one whom a man sends is the equivalent of himself' (Ber. 5:5). The Apostles were men sent by the will of God and commissioned by Jesus to preach and to do mighty works in his name, and in obedience to him.

Jesus had various groups around him. 'The disciples' constitutes the general term which includes 'Apostles' and 'the Twelve'. 'Every Apostle is a disciple but not every disciple an Apostle.'[1] Originally Jesus called the Twelve, primarily to be with him. Then he sent them out, and they became known as Apostles. After the resurrection of Christ, their commission as Apostles was renewed (Matthew 28:16ff). Matthias was appointed in place of the traitor Judas (Acts 1:26). James the Lord's brother was reckoned by Paul as an apostle (Galatians 1:19 cf. 1 Corinthians 15:7). 'The Twelve were the first to receive the Lord's commission, and this encounter with the Risen Lord seems the only ground of apostleship . . . A number of men, specially those who were close to him during his earthly life, received authoritative appointment to be his representatives inside the Christian community. The changed situation made them also missionaries . . .'[2]

Paul was a rather different Apostle. He did not belong to the original circle of the Twelve, nor to the larger group who received their commission shortly after the Resurrection of Christ. None the less he encountered the Risen Lord, and did receive his commission; and, as we have seen, he regarded his status as an apostle as good as 'those reputed pillars of our society' (Galatians 2:9). Indeed he claimed to work harder than the rest in the service of Jesus, even though the fact that he had persecuted the Church made him not worthy to be called an Apostle (1 Corinthians 15:9f).

Paul's apostolic consciousness was completely determined by his encounter with Jesus on the road to Damascus. He speaks of himself, in terms reminiscent of Jeremiah, as being set apart for the Gospel of God from his birth (Romans 1:1; Galatians 1:15). But it was from the time of his *rebirth* that he became conscious of this calling. He sees his apostleship as evidence for the grace of God, for he knows that he did not deserve his calling, but it was simply given him by God.

As an apostle Paul is a servant of God and Jesus Christ, commissioned by him to preach the Gospel of Christ. Paul is not in any way beholden to men for this office. He is 'an apostle not from men neither through a man, but through Jesus Christ' (Galatians 1:1). He therefore does not need the support of men to buttress his claim to apostleship. 'If I still sought men's favour, I should be no servant of Christ.' How does Paul substantiate this claim to the apostolate when he is under attack? He restates his divine appointment. He points to the message of the Cross which he preaches, and to the word of reconciliation. He points to his life-style (1 Corinthians 4:17). He has the Spirit of God (1 Corinthians 7:40). He contrasts with himself 'sham apostles crooked in all their practices, masquerading as apostles of Christ' (2 Corinthians 11:13). In contrast to these 'superlative apostles' he has made known the full truth (2 Corinthians 11:5f). Under pressure he lays claim to the 'works of an apostle' in that his ministry was attended by signs, marvels and miracles (2 Corinthians 12:12). He refers to these elsewhere but always in a minor key, as though they did not lie at the heart of the matter (Romans 15:19;1 Thessalonians 1:5). Strangely enough, he does not seem to put so much weight on the imitation of Christ as in maintaining apostolic witness. True, when writing to the Thessalonians, he says: 'you in your turn followed the example set by us and by the Lord' (1 Thessalonians 1:6), but the Lord takes here second place, and elsewhere he writes more simply: 'Follow my example as I follow Christ's' (1 Corinthians 11:1). Already the cultural difference between Judaea and the Mediterranean basin was such that the imitation of Jesus could not be literally undertaken. The Apostle follows Christ by translating his life-style into the cultural milieu of the Hellenistic world, and Paul bids the churches follow his example. Thus he exercises pastoral care over the flock, 'never ceasing to counsel each of you, night and day' (Acts 20:31).

If Paul saw his own ministry in these terms, how did he see the ministry of others? We must put aside any concept of ordination such as it has evolved today. In Paul's day there were men called to particular offices; there were also informal ministries; and there were of course apostles who held a general ministry. Clearly there were different zones of interest among apostles, just as Paul was called generally to the ministry of Gentiles and Peter to the ministry of Jews (Galatians 2:8).

Although Paul himself spoke with authority and expected his instructions as an Apostle to be obeyed, he held a view of the Church which approximated to later synodical ideals. He writes, to the Corinthians, about a man accused of incest: 'For my part, though I am absent in body, I am present in spirit, and my judgement upon the man who did this thing is already given, as if I were indeed present; you all being assembled in the name of our Lord Jesus Christ, and I with you in spirit, with the power of our Lord Jesus Christ over us . . .' (1

Corinthians 5:3f). Paul takes the decision, but he does it as it were in synod. According to Acts, he appointed elders in each congregation that he founded on his first missionary tour of the cities of what is now Turkey, and there is no good reason to doubt the accuracy of this statement. Obviously the churches had to have leaders, and it would seem natural for Paul to appoint elders. What precisely he meant by this phrase is another matter. Did they correspond exactly to Jewish elders?[3] We cannot be certain. In Acts 20:28, the Ephesian elders are to act as *episcopoi* (overseers), watching over the flock. When Paul and Timothy wrote to the Philippians, they addressed the letter to all who live at Philippi 'including their bishops and deacons' (Philippians 1:1). There is general agreement that these bishops (*episcopoi*) had the same function as the elders of Acts 20:28. Perhaps they are the same as those to whom Paul alludes vaguely as being leaders in the Lord (1 Thessalonians 5:12). It seems that among those to whom he gave responsibility Timothy and Titus held a special place, with general authority to act in his name. We cannot be quite certain whether the Pastoral Epistles reflect a situation during Paul's ministry, or after it; but, on the former assumption, considerable evidence is given in these letters about the qualifications and functions of the ministry, both elders and deacons (1 Timothy 3:1–13). Timothy himself is certainly 'ordained', for Paul reminds him to 'stir up the gift of God which is given him through the laying on of my hands' (2 Timothy 1:6). Timothy is addressed as a kind of deputy by Paul. It is tempting to compare the relationships between them as that of a bishop and archdeacon, but that would be really misleading, for the analogy suggests a settled style of ministry, and the establishment of the 'historic episcopate'; and that is by no means certain. We must not read back the developments of a later age into the primitive Church. There has been much debate whether the ministry evolved 'upwards' from elders to the monarchical bishop, or 'downwards' from the Apostles and Apostolic men; and although no certainty can be attained, the truth seems likely to be a combination of both.[4] There is little doubt that the Apostle Paul appointed elders and leaders in the churches which he founded, and it would have been most irresponsible not to have done so. But nobody knows whether these, and these only, presided at the Lord's Supper, or whether they could authorize or 'license' anyone else to preside. What happened for example in Colossae? Paul had never visited there. Epaphras, his 'dear fellow servant' (Colossians 1:17) was a trusted worker 'on our behalf'. Tychicus, another trusted fellow servant, is bringing news to the Colossians of Paul's affairs (Colossians 4:7). Paul seems to know many of the Christians there, to judge from his greetings at the end of his letter. At the same time, we have no idea what arrangements had been made for ministry in the church at Colossae, and by whom. We do not know whether elders were appointed by the laying on of hands as a result of the ministry of Paul's fellow missionaries.

There are however a few passages where Paul gives his views about ministry in general. In the Epistle to the Ephesians there is a theological discussion about the relationship of the apostolic ministry to ministry as a whole and to the person of Christ. Jesus is raised from the dead so as to 'fill the universe'. His presence, no longer localized, is universal. But although Christ was no longer localized and particularized, his gifts to his Church were very precise, at least so far as ministry is concerned. According to Paul in this passage, he gave four orders of ministry, of which the apostles are pre-eminent. The reason for this ministry is 'to equip God's people in his service, to the building up of the body of Christ. So shall we all attain to the unity inherent in our faith and our knowledge of the Son of

God – to mature manhood, measured by nothing less than the full stature of Christ' (Ephesians 4:12f). There is no doubt in Paul's mind about the pre-eminence of apostles – they take pride of place over prophets, evangelists, pastors and teachers. None the less 'as the Ministry is a function of the Church, so the Church is a function of the Kingdom, of the Universal Lordship of God in Christ'.[5] In an earlier passage, Paul speaks in not dissimilar terms about the ministry of *totus Christus* as a function of the Church. Writing to the Corinthians, who are disposed to divisions, Paul emphasizes the need for all people, with their differing gifts, to work together. He is concerned about the total Christian ministry. He writes: 'Now you are Christ's body and each of you a limb or organ of it. Within our community, God has appointed, in the first place, apostles, in the second place prophets, thirdly teachers; then miracle workers, then those who have gifts of healing, or ability to help others or power to guide them, or gifts of ecstatic utterance of various kinds.' 'Are all apostles?' he asks (1 Corinthians 12: 27ff). Here Paul speaks of 'informal' as well as 'recognized' ministries.

In neither of these lists are deacons mentioned although in Philippians they seem to comprise a recognized category, as indeed later was the case. The lists of ministries in the Epistle to the Romans and 1 Corinthians differ, but apostles have pride of place in both. Paul never minimizes his calling. Paul is aware of the great authority which God has bestowed upon him and which Christ has given him.[6] He gives weight to the ministry of prophets,[7] but he makes it quite clear that all other ministries in the Church are subservient to his. Paul does not always exercise his apostleship in a spirit of meekness. He writes in a somewhat exasperated way to the disloyal Corinthians: 'The kingdom of God is not a matter of talk, but of power. Choose, then; am I to come to you with a rod in my hand, or in love and a gentle spirit?' (1 Corinthians 4:21). He must have been sorely tried!

We might perhaps have expected Paul to quote some words of the Lord Jesus about ministry. For example, Jesus made it clear that, in contrast to those who held authority in the world, he came not to be served but to serve (Mark 10:45). Jesus would not tell people where his authority lay (Mark 11:33). As for his deputies and representatives, Jesus is recorded as saying: 'Whoever receives one of these children in my name, receives me; and whoever receives me receives not me but the One who sent me' (Mark 9:37). Was Jesus interested in founding a Church?[8] Paul certainly was. He seemed to be not interested in the words of the Lord about ministry. Perhaps he would have seen the situation as radically altered from that of Jesus's ministry. We have no means of knowing whether Paul knew Jesus during the period of his public ministry before the Crucifixion. According to Acts, he studied under Gamaliel, presumably in Jerusalem. Paul does not write of what Jesus said or did during this period. However, he knows the salient facts about Jesus's life, his Crucifixion and Resurrection. In his ethical teaching there are both some direct quotations from Jesus's teaching, or evident allusions. He also shows knowledge of personal attitudes of Jesus, such as his forgiveness.[9] We have to remember the 'occasional' nature of the extant letters of Paul. In writing to churches perhaps we should not expect more than echoes of the ministry of Jesus and occasional references to his teaching. He may not have thought that this was relevant to the changed circumstances of life in the early Church compared with Jesus's ministry in Galilee, Samaria and Judaea. In any case Paul had not become aware of his call to the apostolate until after those days were over. His allegiance was not to Jesus but to the Risen Lord, and he had to deal with situations in the Hellenistic Church far removed from those with which Jesus was confronted during his ministry in Galilee and Judaea.

Paul was never conscious of being an innovator. Although he speaks about 'my gospel' (Romans 2:16), he does not write possessively. When he writes of 'another Gospel' (2 Corinthians 11:4; Galatians 1:6), he refers to false teaching by his opponents rather than to the Christian traditions held by the churches as a whole. In fact he is keen to pass on to the Corinthians 'the facts which had been imparted to me' concerning the death and resurrection of Christ (1 Corinthians 15:3), and similarly he passes on 'from the Lord himself' the tradition he has received concerning the institution of the Eucharist (1 Corinthians 11:23).

If Paul was not an innovator, can we with any certainty recover from the New Testament the Gospel which others were preaching in Paul's day? An attempt has been made to do just this, by examining the early speeches in the Acts of the Apostles, and comparing these with what Paul writes. Of course the question is raised whether these early speeches are the invention of Luke, or whether they reflect the primitive preaching of the Gospel.[10] On the whole the arguments seem to favour authenticity. The early preaching or *kerygma* seems to have been as follows: Jesus was foretold by the prophets of old. He went about doing good and healing all kinds of sickness among the people. He was wrongly put to death by the Jews, crucified on a cross of wood. God raised him from the dead, and exalted him to his right hand in heaven. After his ascension, the Holy Spirit was poured out among men. Therefore, said the Apostles, people must repent and be baptized.

This seems to have been the common preaching (*kerygma*) of the primitive Church, as distinguished from its teaching (*didache*), which concerned Christian behaviour. Originally the preaching seems to have been strong on affirmation but weak on interpretation. An interpretation was already present in germ, but it needed to flower. For example, the early Church felt strongly that the death of Jesus had a special significance. As time went on, various interpretations were sketched in. The death of Jesus began to be understood in the Church as a sacrifice, a ransom-price, a redemption and emancipation, a victory, a justification. Paul had a brilliant and original mind, and so his interpretation was most original and forceful.[11] But it must not be thought that his was different from other early Christian thinkers. The First Epistle of Peter and the Epistle to the Hebrews are sometimes included among what used to be called 'Deutero-Pauline' literature, because they are in some ways similar to Paul in thinking. But 'Deutero-Pauline' begs the question of their date. Those who hold, like myself, that 1 Peter emanated from the Chief of the Apostles,[12] will see a development here not dissimilar from that of Paul – not altogether surprising, if Silvanus, who is associated with Peter in writing it, is the same person as the Silas who at one stage accompanied Paul. Again, it is fashionable to put the composition of the Epistle to the Hebrews at a time after the Fall of Jerusalem in A.D. 70. Those who date this Epistle early, as I do, would see here as brilliant and equally original an interpretation of Jesus's death as Paul produced in his Justification Theory.[13]

When was Paul converted to Christ? Here I would like to quote some words of Professor C. H. Dodd:

His conversion can, on his own showing, be dated not later than A.D. 33–34. His first visit to Jerusalem was three years after this (possibly just over two years on our exclusive reckoning); at the most therefore not more than seven years after the crucifixion. At that time he stayed with Peter for a fortnight, and we assume they did not spend all the time talking about the weather. After that he had no direct contact with the primitive Church for fourteen years, that is to say, almost down to the period to which our epistles belong, and it is difficult to see how he could during this time have had any opportunity of further instruction in the apostolic traditions.

The date therefore, at which Paul received the fundamentals of the Gospel cannot well be later than some seven years after the death of Jesus Christ. It may be earlier, and indeed, we must assume some knowledge of the tenets of Christianity in Paul even before his conversion. Thus Paul's preaching represents a special stream of Christian tradition which was derived from the main stream at a point very near to its source. No doubt his own idiosyncracy counted for much in his presentation of the Gospel, but anyone who should maintain that the primitive Christian Gospel was fundamentally different from that which we have found in Paul must bear the burden of proof.[14]

That proof has not been forthcoming.

If we attempt to trace the apostolic labours of Paul, we must begin first with his own autobiographical details such as can be culled from his extant letters. Fortunately for us, his controversy with false teachers among the churches of Galatia is such that he is forced to explain his own position, which he does in an autobiographical sketch, written on oath. Again, the crisis of authority which he suffered in Corinth was such that, once again, more personal details are produced. However, if it were not for the Acts of the Apostles it would not be possible to give a convincing account of his journeys, or to indicate the places from which he wrote to the various churches which he had founded.

Here however lies a twofold difficulty. In the first place, there are matters recounted in the Acts which are very hard to make tally with the situation in the Epistles

– for example the Council at Jerusalem in Acts 15 does not seem to correspond with anything in the Epistles, and it seems so important, in view of Paul's problems with Judaizers, that one wonders how Paul did not mention it, if it ever took place. Again, his private visit recounted in Galatians cannot be made to tally as it stands with any of the visits recorded in Acts. Apart from these points there are problems in ascribing Acts to Luke at all; and there are scholars who regard it as a much later work.[15] If this is so, its value as a historical work is further diminished. My own view is that it should be attributed to Luke, but (as can be seen in his treatment of the Synoptic tradition) Luke sat fairly light to historical accuracy, and made it subservient to his main objectives in writing. What does this mean for trying to reconstruct Paul's apostolic labours? It is probably best to assume the accuracy of the Acts except for particular events or situations the historicity of which there is good reason, from Paul's letters, to doubt. Since the preface to Acts stakes out a claim to accuracy, it is fair to assume that the author restricts within limits his liberty of reshaping the story.

Bearing this in mind, we may proceed to attempt to reconstruct Paul's career as an Apostle. But first the general situation of the Church must be considered, before we can see how he made his own particular contribution. We may divide the expansion of the Christian Church into three stages.

The first was centred on Jerusalem. Large numbers joined what must then have been regarded as a Jewish sect, differing from the rest of Judaism in believing not that the Messiah would come, but that he had come and that his own people had rejected him. Although at this stage the Church grew among Jews within Judaea and Galilee, non-Jews also were included, such as the Samaritans whom Philip had converted and whose entry Peter and John had confirmed (Acts 8); and also Cornelius, whose baptism Peter had authorized, which the Apostles and members of the Church in Judaea had subsequently ratified (Acts 10f). These conversions were the result of the scattering of Christians from Jerusalem into the country districts of Judaea and Samaria (Acts 8:1).

The second phase of the Church's expansion began with a further persecution, which scattered Christians far beyond the area of Judaea, as a result of the trouble that Stephen had caused (Acts 11:19). This persecution arose within two or three years of the death of Jesus, and according to Acts Paul was one of those who had supported the martyrdom of Stephen (Acts 8:1). During this second phase Christians made their way to Antioch (where they first were called Christians),[16] as well as to Phoenicia and Cyprus (Acts 11:19). At first they preached only to Jews, but Gentiles soon were included and accepted as believers (Acts 11:20). Probably at this time there were Christians in Rome as well, for when Paul wrote his Epistle to the Romans, he assumed that there was a well established Church there. If so, Christianity was during this second phase established in the largest cities of the Roman Empire, in Rome the capital, and at Antioch one of the great cities of the Empire. At this point the centre of Christianity was still with the mother church at Jerusalem, over which James the Lord's brother seems to have ruled as head, while the Apostles made visitations to the various churches. Peter is mentioned by Paul as visiting both Corinth and Antioch (1 Corinthians 3:22; Galatians 2:11), and the Apostles and the Lord's brothers actually drew travelling allowances for their wives (1 Corinthians 9:5)! It was of course during this second phase that Paul was converted, as he was trying to stamp out the Christian movement in Damascus.

The third and final phase before A.D. 70 began when the church at Antioch took the initiative in missionary work. Barnabas had been sent earlier to Antioch by the

Jerusalem church to see whether the church there had been acting foolishly in admitting Gentiles to its fellowship. Barnabas was so impressed by what he saw that, after reporting back to Jerusalem, he returned to Antioch, and then went off to Tarsus to fetch Paul (Acts 11:26). We may assume that this was around A.D. 45. Paul on his own admission (after his conversion about A.D. 33), had disappeared into Arabia shortly afterwards. He then returned to Damascus, and, we may surmise, had returned to his native city of Tarsus when Barnabas sought him out there. He himself tells us that he 'went to the regions of Syria and Cilicia' (Galatians 1:21) and Tarsus was in the neighbourhood.

It was during this third phase of the Church's expansion that Paul went on his missionary journeys. No doubt the author of Acts gives special emphasis to Paul as a missionary, partly because he had accompanied Paul on some of these journeys (if the 'We Passages' in Acts are part of a genuine travel document),[17] and partly because Paul was his hero and he balances his Petrine stories with those about Paul. There must have been many other Christian missionaries spreading the Gospel around Asia Minor and even in Greece, as some remarks of Paul suggest (cf. 2 Corinthians 10:13). The opening verse of 1 Peter addresses churches which may well have been during this period the churches established by such unknown missionaries. But the mother church at Jerusalem still had a special place in the affections of these Christians, just as the Jews themselves looked to Jerusalem and sent their annual tribute money to the upkeep of the Temple.

After A.D. 70, however, all this changed. The Jewish Temple was destroyed. Jews could no longer make their annual pilgrimages for the Great Festivals. The temple tax went to the Roman authorities. Similarly for Christians Jerusalem ceased to be the centre of their movement. The Church in Jerusalem simply ceased to exist. According to the church historian Eusebius, Christians had moved out to Pella before the capital fell to the Romans.[18]After that catastrophic event the distinctively Jewish Christians disappeared from sight. Occasionally tantalizing glimpses of them are found in the early Fathers, and in fragments from the Gospel of the Hebrews.[19] Pauline Christianity became the reigning orthodoxy, and no doubt took good care to see that the documents of Jewish Christianity (such as were castigated by Paul in the Epistle to the Galatians) were suppressed.[20]

Paul's missionary work fell within the third of the three phases of Christian expanses prior to A.D. 70. About A.D. 47 he was sent out by the Church of Antioch together with Barnabas and Mark, and they went to Cyprus. From there Paul and Barnabas went on to Asia, to Perga, Pisidonian Antioch, Iconium, Lystra, Derbe and back to Antioch in late A.D. 48. This is his first missionary journey. Then, according to Acts 15, they were both sent to Jerusalem to get the question of circumcision for Gentile believers settled (in A.D. 48). They then returned back to Antioch with (according to Acts) a very liberal settlement.

When back at Antioch it occurred to Paul that he ought to revisit the churches which he had founded in Asia, and together with Silas he set off in A.D. 49, going to Derbe and Lystra, and 'they travelled through the Phrygian and Galatian region, because they were prevented by the Holy Spirit from delivering the message in the province of Asia' (Acts 16:6). (The interpretation of this passage is not really clear.) When Paul came to the seaport of Troas, he had a vision which caused him to cross over to Greece. There he stayed at Philippi, and went on to Thessalonika, where he stayed about three weeks, before being forced on to Beroea, and then on again to Athens. He left Athens and went to Corinth, where he stayed for some eighteen months.

Passing through Ephesus he made his way to Jerusalem, paid his respects to the church there and then got back to Antioch in A.D. 51, thus ending his second missionary journey.

From Antioch Paul went on his third voyage, overland to Ephesus, where he stayed for three whole years until A.D. 55, and became a well known person throughout the province. After a riot at Ephesus he had to leave there too, and he went to Macedonia and Greece to revisit the churches that he had founded there, returning to Ephesus, and then setting out for the last time to Jerusalem in A.D. 57. He had had a premonition that all would not go well with him there, and indeed his opponents from the province of Asia saw him in the Temple apparently going through rites of purification. (If this is historical, it casts an interesting light on Paul's personal adherence to the Jewish law.) During the resulting riot, Paul was arrested, taken to Caesarea, where he stayed for two years until A.D. 59, and finally as a result of 'appealing to Caesar' to have his case heard in Rome (a privilege accorded to Roman citizens), he finally made his way to the capital of the Empire, arriving in A.D. 60, after exciting adventures.

What happened to him after that is lost in legend. He is thought by some to have gone to Spain as he said he hoped to do (Romans 15:23). He is said to have been martyred in Rome together with Peter during the Neronian persecution. His end is unknown to history.

We may perhaps summarize Paul's time as an Apostle as follows:

1. Conversion   A.D. 33

2. First Jerusalem Visit   ,,   35

3. 2nd (Famine) Visit   ,,   35

This chronology is much debated, in so far as there are some uncertainties not least in reconciling this outline in Acts with the visits to Jerusalem which he records in the Epistle to the Galatians.[21]

There follows the puzzle of determining just when his extant letters were written. Much time has been spent on this literary and historical puzzle. It naturally adds to our understanding of this correspondence if we know the situation which elicited it. However there is very little evidence other than that found in Acts and in the Epistles which is relevant to fixing the dates of these letters, and so far as their *religious* value is concerned, the date, place of origin and place of destination of these letters is comparatively unimportant. For example, it makes very little difference to the *religious value* of the Epistle to the Galatians whether it was written to the churches of South or North Galatia! Similarly it does not affect the religious value of the Epistle to the Ephesians whether it was addressed to the church at Ephesus, or was a pastoral letter sent to many churches, one of which was Ephesus.

But some points are vital. For example, it makes a

great difference to our understanding of 2 Corinthians if we think that the present letter was written as a complete Epistle, or that it is made up of two letters and a fragment of a third. What of the Pastoral Epistles? In the past the question of their authenticity has engendered much heat. Is this a vital point too? Since everyone agrees that if they were not written by Paul they were certainly written by a Paulinist, their date makes little difference to their religious value, except that we may perhaps doubt the abiding worth of letters purporting to be written by someone but in fact composed after that person had died.

The whole question of dating New Testament documents is very difficult. There is little reliable evidence other than that of the documents. Lately the question has been re-opened by a powerful book which argues cogently for earlier dates than have usually been acceptable to critical scholarship.[22] In a short study such as this there is little point in entering into the detailed arguments on either side.

Nobody knows how the existing letters of Paul were collected, but an attractive theory has been put forward.[23] It is based on the fact that Paul wrote a personal letter to Philemon, who lived in Asia Minor, the only fragment of personal correspondence which survives from the hand of the Apostle. Paul wrote this letter on behalf of a runaway slave called Onesimus who had turned up in Rome, and whom Paul had converted and sent back to his former master, who was also a Christian. Paul writes most tactfully, and asks Philemon to treat Onesimus well. Now a certain Onesimus became Bishop of Ephesus in the sub-apostolic age. The suggestion has been made that when the Acts of the Apostles were published and reached Ephesus, Onesimus, feeling that Paul had not been recognized by the Christian churches as he should have been, wrote round to the churches which Paul, according to Acts, had founded, and asked them whether they had in their archives any letters from Paul. (It will be noted that all extant letters are addressed to places mentioned in the Acts as visited by Paul.) It has been suggested that Onesimus by these means collected the Pauline corpus and prefaced it with something of his own composition, the Epistle to the Ephesians, so as to give a penetrating introduction to Pauline thought, although it was in reality Onesimus's composition. This would account for the existence of one private letter in the New Testament, the Epistle to Philemon about Onesimus.

This is an attractive theory; but it is based on pure supposition and makes many assumptions that would not find general acceptance. It assumes that the Pastoral Epistles were not from the Apostle's hand, and likewise the Epistle to the Ephesians. It also assumes that 2 Peter could not come from the hand of Peter, because the hypothesis requires that the Pauline corpus must have been collected after Peter died, and yet the collection had already been made and published by the time 2 Peter was written. For we find the following in that Epistle:

> Bear in mind that our Lord's patience with us is our salvation, as Paul, our friend and brother, said when he wrote to you with his inspired wisdom. And so he does in all his other letters, wherever he speaks on this subject, though they contain some obscure passages, which the ignorant and unstable misinterpret to their own ruin, as they do the other scriptures.
> (2 Peter 3:15ff).

The theory gives an attractive explanation of how the Pauline letters could have been collected, but it must be regarded as unproven, or even rejected, if only for the assumptions on which it rests.

Those who have investigated the matter are divided

about whether the collection of Paul's letters was made gradually, or whether the complete collection was made at once. They are divided also about whether the original collection consisted of the present thirteen letters, or whether the Pastoral Epistles were added later. This is a complex subject, and unsuitable for detailed examination here.[24] It is also uncertain whether the present collection consists of all those letters which then survived, or whether it represents a selection from the huge number of letters which the Apostle must have written. The present order of the letters does not represent the original order as known to Marcion in the early Church; but the significance of that order is unknown. It is unfortunate that we are surrounded in this matter by such a large area of uncertainty but it is always best to acknowledge the limitations of our knowledge on New Testament matters. Dr Mitton, who has investigated this subject in some depth, believes that three conclusions can be named which are probable, even if they do not achieve the level of complete certainty.[25] They are these:

1. The letters of Paul sprang suddenly into the life of the Christian community, about a generation after they had been written, and in such a way as to suggest that they had been deliberately collected and then published as a corpus, after a considerable period of almost complete neglect.
2. This collection took place about A.D. 90.
3. It was carried into effect in or near Ephesus.

To these letters we now turn.

3   PAUL THE WRITER

There are nine surviving letters of Paul to particular churches, one private letter, and three 'pastoral letters' to Timothy and Titus. This must be only a minute fraction of the total number of letters that Paul wrote. After all there lay upon him 'the care of all the churches' (2 Corinthians 11:28). If he could not be everywhere at once, he could at least communicate regularly with the churches by letter when he could not send a personal emissary. He dictated his own letters, and at the end of the Epistle to the Romans there is a charming little addendum: 'I Tertius, who took this letter down, add my Christian greetings' (Romans 16:22). Unfortunately it was possible then as now for letters to be forged, so that Paul wrote to the Thessalonians of 'some letter purporting to come from us' (2 Thessalonians 2:2). To counter such missives, Paul signed with his own hand (2 Thessalonians 3:17), sometimes drawing attention to the extra large script which he used (Galatians 6:11). (This is hardly evidence of his bad eyesight!) Sometimes he asked that a letter he had written to one church should be read elsewhere, as when the Colossians were invited to send their letter to the Laodiceans to be read in their church, and the Laodicean letter (which no longer survives) in turn to be read in Colossae (Colossians 4:16). Paul was a lettered man who valued his library. There is something touching about the message to Timothy: 'When you come, bring the cloak I left with Carpus at Troas, and the books, and above all my notebooks' (2 Timothy 4:13).

Without Paul's letters we would know little about the character of the man, his frustrations and his encouragements, his friends and his enemies. We would be totally reliant on the information that is given in the Acts of the Apostles, with the tantalizing statement in 2 Peter about how hard his letters were to understand (2 Peter 3:16).

Paul's language is usually very precise. It is only when attempting to translate an Epistle into modern English that one realizes just how precise Paul is, and how many nuances there are in his Greek text. I found this when I was helping to prepare a diglot 'translation for translators' for the British and Foreign Bible Society.[1] I discovered all kinds of nuances and allusions in 1 Corinthians which I had never realized were there when studying an English translation, or using a commentary on the Greek text. Paul's Greek is adequate, without being distinguished. He is not a writer of good Greek, like Luke, nor does he produce the elegant and stylish Greek of the rigorous-minded author of the Epistle to the Hebrews. He is a forceful writer, and he will use any word or phrase that conveys his meaning with force and clarity. Studies have been done on his preference for certain words, and on the length of his sentences,[2] in order to attempt to distinguish genuine letters from those which are Pseudepigraphical. However, the length of a sentence is not so easy to determine in Greek as in English, for there is no punctuation in the ancient manuscripts. As for an author's language, different words and phrases may be used in differing situations, and at different times in a person's life. Paul wrote as someone who knew Hebrew, as well as being familiar with the Greek Bible (the Septuagint). His lingua franca was not classical Greek, but *Koine*, the Hellenistic Greek of his day. Much light has been shed on the meaning of what Paul wrote by a study of papyrus fragments;[3] and deductions have even been made about certain epistles from the average length of a papyrus roll![4]

Paul's letters are printed among the New Testament

epistles not in their chronological order but according to their length;[5] and it is in that order that they are considered below.[6]

THE EPISTLE TO THE ROMANS

This is Paul's most substantial letter, both in length and content.[7] Although he had often planned to visit the church in Rome, he had always been frustrated (Romans 1:13). He evidently had taken particular pains to compose a full statement of his beliefs when writing to the church in the capital of the Roman Empire. Already in his day this was a church of influence and importance, and because it was a non-Pauline foundation, Paul felt that it was particularly important to set out his Christian faith more fully and systematically than in any of his other surviving epistles.

As so often with his other letters, the Epistle to the Romans may be dated and placed in its context by means of the personal references in the letter. When Paul wrote, he was on his way to Jerusalem 'on an errand to God's people there' (Romans 15:25). He intended to deliver the collection he had made 'under my own seal' at the mother church of Jerusalem. At the time of writing he was staying with Gaius in Corinth, whom he had baptized when he founded the church there (1 Corinthians 1:14) and whom he now described as 'my host and the host of the whole congregation' – presumably the Corinthian church met in his house. According to Acts 20:3, Paul spent three months in Achaia before he started for Jerusalem, and the Epistle may therefore be dated with some confidence in A.D. 57.

There are literary problems concerning the last two chapters. It seems that the Epistle may have circulated at one stage without them, and also without the references to Rome in the first chapter. The suggestion has been made that chapter 16, with its many references to

individuals, is unlikely to have been written by Paul to a
church which he had never visited, and it may therefore
be a covering letter, sent with the Epistle to a destination
such as Ephesus. But Paul is likely to have had many
friends in the capital. It is probably best to assume that
Paul wrote the letter substantially as we have it.
Marcion, a second century heretic who cut down the
New Testament ruthlessly and who thereby helped to
cause the canon of Scripture to be formed, probably
used a shorter version of it.

The argument of the Epistle is in large part
reproduced in a later chapter of this book where Paul's
theology is examined. The Epistle sets out Paul's beliefs
on creation, fall and redemption, with particular
reference to the Jewish Law. It also includes, in chapters
9–11, a valuable section on the purpose of God in
history. This traces the election of Israel, and the
survival of a 'remnant' to be the bearer of God's
revelation. It deals also with Paul's deepest convictions
about his own race, the Jews. He cannot believe that
God has finally rejected his own chosen people. His
heart remains with them, for all that he is called to work
predominantly among non-Jews. 'I am a missionary to
the Gentiles, and as such I give all honour to that
ministry when I try to stir emulation in the men of my
own race, and so to save some of them' (11:13). He
believes that, only after the Gentiles had been admitted
in full strength, would the whole of Israel be saved
(11:25f). He seems therefore to look forward in the end
to universal salvation, although it is perhaps not fair to
expect a firm and settled conviction from Paul on a
matter on which so many have vacillated. At the end of
this section, Paul's heart overcomes his head, and he
bursts out: 'O depth of wealth, wisdom and knowledge
in God! How unsearchable his judgements, how
untraceable his ways . . .' (11:33ff).

The Epistle also contains, towards the end, a

particularly valuable passage on Christian behaviour, and the need for Christian forbearance towards those who conscientiously differ in matters of practice. In such matters Paul shows himself above all as a pastor. He is more concerned with helping to build up the common life of Christians than to lay down an inflexible code of behaviour for all to follow. Never far from his mind are the potential divisions between Jewish and Gentile Christians. 'Accept one another,' he begs them, 'as Christ accepted us' (15:7).

FIRST EPISTLE TO THE CORINTHIANS

Paul founded the church at Corinth in A.D. 50 when he stayed in the city for three months earning his living as a tentmaker, during his second missionary journey. Not as large and prestigious as Ephesus or Antioch, nor as learned as Alexandria, Corinth was still one of the great cities of the ancient world. Its geographical position on the isthmus between the Peloponnese and the Greek mainland gave it a strategic importance. Although a Greek city with a Roman governor, its people were cosmopolitan, with an unenviable reputation for immorality and depravity. It was also a considerable centre of trade and learning.

Paul wrote 1 Corinthians from Ephesus in A.D. 55, towards the end of his three-year stay there. He had kept in touch with the city during the intervening years – not a difficult feat between two great sea ports. In fact, he had actually written an earlier letter to Corinth, instructing the congregation to have nothing to do with loose-livers (1 Corinthians 5:9). It is possible that a fragment of this letter still survives in 2 Corinthians 6:14–7:1, a passage on this very theme which does not fit well in its present context. It is also possible that this 'previous letter' contained the very points which were subsequently dealt with in the written letter from

Corinth which was brought to Paul at Ephesus by the hands of Stephanas, Fortunatus and Achaicus (1 Corinthians 16:17). Paul seems to tick off his answers to the Corinthians' written points with the introductory formula 'Now concerning the . . .' The envoys from Corinth also brought Paul an up-to-date picture of the Corinthian situation and evidently furnished him with particulars on other matters as well. In addition 'Chloe's people' (whoever they were) brought Paul news of the serious state of the church at Corinth by reason of its internal divisions (1 Corinthians 1:11). There were partisans of Paul, of Peter and of Apollos, and also a 'holy' group ('I am Christ's'). No doubt Paul had other informants and other sources of information as well, which he does not specify. The situation was sufficiently serious for him to write a long reply on all the matters about which the Corinthians were in need of guidance or correction.

The result is the letter which we know as 1 Corinthians. It gives us an unparalleled insight into the pastoral, doctrinal and moral problems of the early Church. It confronts us with some of the challenges of Hellenistic thought with which the Gospel had to deal in a cosmopolitan centre like Corinth. It shows us the moral issues facing Christians recently converted from an amoral pagan way of life. The number of matters with which the Apostle has to deal here is astonishing. He writes with warmth and pastoral care, and his style is vivid and lively.

The written letter from Corinth seems to have contained questions about associating with loose-livers, marriage, the celibate, idol meats, 'spiritual men', the veiling of women, bodily resurrection, Paul's collection for the poor at Jerusalem, and Apollos. Other matters which Paul heard about, but which are not mentioned in the letter from Corinth, seem to have included the party divisions about which Chloe's people told him, the case of an incestuous man, and the divisions which took place at church assemblies, especially at and before the commemoration of the Lord's Supper during common meals. Paul also seems to have realized (from some undisclosed source) that Corinthian Christians were having recourse to pagan magistrates to settle their differences, and that they were claiming freedom from all moral restraint as a result of their new-found liberty in Christ. It is fascinating that so many of these problems were to recur during the history of Christendom; yet they all had to be faced within twenty-five years of the death and resurrection of Jesus!

THE SECOND EPISTLE TO THE CORINTHIANS

Paul's letter did not settle the affair. Indeed, much worse was to come. We can learn more from 2 Corinthians about what happened after the receipt of 1 Corinthians than we can from the compressed account in Acts. Paul had despatched Timothy to Corinth before writing 1 Corinthians (1 Corinthians 4:17), but he did not know whether he had yet arrived (16:10). News then reached Paul that there was a grave crisis of authority in the Corinthian church. Further steps were necessary. He sent Titus (2 Corinthians 12:18), but he was beside himself with worry. He must go himself. Paul made a second visit to Corinth. The journey from one great port to another would not have been difficult. It was a most distressing visit, and Paul made up his mind that a third visit must not be 'another painful one' like the second (2 Corinthians 2:1). Paul refused to accept any travelling allowance for this visit (12:13), which was a total disaster. Paul's authority was at stake – and he was humiliated. His opponents had won. In particular there was one offender who had quite overstepped the mark (2:5).

Paul retired to Corinth hurt and baffled. Whatever could he do now? He could write a letter. He was better on paper than face to face – he knew that. And a letter he wrote, arguing, pleading, wheedling, threatening; what he calls a 'severe letter'. What a time he had writing it! 'That letter I sent you came out of great distress and anxiety; how many tears I shed as I wrote it!' It was a wounding letter (2 Corinthians 7:8f), even if he protests that he never meant to hurt, but only that the Corinthians should know that the love he had for them was more than ordinary love (2:5). It was written from Ephesus in A.D. 56. This severe letter is probably incorporated in the present 2 Corinthians, and forms chapters 10:1–13:10. As they stand, these chapters, with their strongly critical tone, make no sense coming after the first nine chapters which breathe quite a different atmosphere. They fit very well with just what we would have expected in a severe letter, and many of the points made in them seem to be taken up in chapters 1–9, assuming that these belong to a later letter.

Paul did not know the outcome of this severe letter. He had several times in it threatened a third visit to the Corinthians. He did not however make this visit directly – he simply could not face a further humiliation. And so he went off to Troas, where he found that evangelical opportunities opened up before him (2 Corinthians 2:12). But even this could not calm him: he was so worried about what was happening in Corinth. Titus had been there. He hoped that Titus would come and tell him the outcome; but there was only silence. Was no news good news? Paul did not know, but he feared the worst. He was so restless that he left Troas and went off to Macedonia (2:12–14). And when he got to Macedonia there was still silence from Corinth. There was 'trouble at every turn, quarrels all round us, forebodings in our heart' (7:15).

And then the news came – and what news! 'God, who

brings comfort to the downcast, has comforted us by the arrival of Titus, and not merely by his arrival, but by his being so greatly comforted about you. He has told me how you long for me, how sorry you are, and how eager to take my side; and that has made me happier still' (2 Corinthians 7:6f). A miracle had happened. Out of disaster had come complete success. Out of the worst had come the best. Paul's mood changed abruptly. He wrote to the Corinthians a paean of praise and thanksgiving, forgiving his opponents and exulting in the reconciliation that had been effected. And this joyful letter is to be found in 2 Corinthians 1–9 (apart from the fragment 2 Corinthians 6:14–7:1). This too was written in A.D. 56, from Macedonia.

Is this division of 2 Corinthians into three parts at all credible? Perhaps we may reconstruct a situation at Corinth years later, near the beginning of the second century, when a search was being made in the church archives for Paul's letters sent to Corinth long, long before. The first letter to the Corinthians had been known in Rome before the end of the century, for Clement of Rome quotes from it. Had Corinth any more letters from the venerable Apostle? Three papyrus rolls may have been found, one a complete letter, one part of a letter, one a fragment. No one quite knew to what they referred. It would have been easy to join them up, and to add the ending of the first letter to the end of what was now a single papyrus roll. The second letter to the Corinthians is not cited by the early Fathers until the middle of the second century. Perhaps it had not been joined into one letter long before.

THE EPISTLE TO THE GALATIANS

This letter, like 1 Peter, is not addressed to a particular church but to a group of churches; in this case 'to the

Christian churches of Galatia' (Galatians 1:2). This however is a somewhat ambiguous term. Galatia could refer to the ancient country of Galatia, a broad strip of land, some two hundred miles long, stretching from north-east to south-west in the interior of Asia Minor. Alternatively it could refer to the Roman province of Galatia, formed by Augustus, and comprising not only ancient Galatia, but also Lycaonia (including Derbe and Lystra), Isauria, and parts of Phrygia and Pisidia. It is clear that Paul has already visited the congregations addressed in this Epistle, because he is surprised at the speed with which their members have changed his Gospel for a different Judaizing Gospel (Galatians 1:6f). Paul wrote, 'As you know it was bodily illness that in the first place led me to bring you the Gospel' (Galatians 4:13). The word translated in the first place (Greek *proteron*) can mean either 'on the first of two occasions' or 'formerly'; that is to say, the word is compatible with Paul having visited these churches either once or twice before he wrote to them. This does not make dating any easier! It has been suggested that Paul went to the northern uplands of the ancient country of Galatia to convalesce after a serious illness. But it seems more likely that Paul was referring to the Roman province, although no proof is possible and we can only surmise. If so, he was writing to the churches he had founded on his second missionary journey. If he had visited them only once before he wrote, Galatians was probably written from somewhere like Ephesus in A.D. 56. An earlier date would be A.D. 47, after Paul's first missionary journey, but before the Jerusalem Council which settled the terms on which Gentile Christians could be received into the Church – a matter with which Galatians is mostly concerned. We need not, however, expect Paul to quote from the Council in a later letter to Galatian churches, for the Jerusalem Council was specifically for Antioch, Syria and Cilicia, and there would have been little point in citing this local edict in a later controversy elsewhere. The Epistle has marked affinities in style and content with the Epistle to the Romans, and also some possible links with 1 Corinthians. In view of this it seems best to assume that it was written by Paul from Ephesus in A.D. 56, the later date, a year after the Epistle to the Romans and around the same time as the Corinthian correspondence. But there is not the same certainty here as with the other letters we have considered. As we have seen, it could be much earlier than A.D.56; it could even have been later. Paul writes of 'the instructions he has given to congregations in Galatia' about the collection (1 Corinthians 16:1), but the collection is not mentioned in Galatians. This might suggest either that the letter was written before Paul had thought of the collection, or that it was penned after the collection had been made. But Paul was writing in white heat about circumcision, and the collection probably never entered his head!

Whenever the letter was actually written, the situation to which it is addressed is clear. Judaizers were insisting that Gentile converts should be circumcized. This for Paul was a 'different Gospel' for it went right across his deepest convictions about God accepting people not because of their achievements, but through their faith in the atoning death of Christ. He used many arguments (some of them reminiscent of the Epistle to the Romans) to prove his point, and it is clear that his emotions as much as his intellect were deeply engaged. The Epistle is written in a warm and characteristic style and contains an invaluable autobiographical section.

THE EPISTLE TO THE EPHESIANS

This Epistle is one of those which has not universally been attributed to Paul. Objections have been raised to the vocabulary, to the style and to length of sentences, and even the use of the Greek word 'and' (*kai*). There is a marked similarity between the Epistle to the Ephesians and the Epistle to the Colossians. The resemblances are so close and yet the differences in meaning are so great that it is difficult to imagine someone concocting one from the other. The Epistle to the Colossians contains a host of personal references, but the Epistle to the Ephesians only one such reference, to Tychicus, in exactly the same words as the reference in Colossians. It is easy enough to find difficulties in attributing Ephesians to Paul – the style is more elevated, the argument accumulative rather than dialectical, the vocabulary at times different, the sentences longer – yet it is even more difficult to make a credible case for a Paulinist compiler concocting the letter. Why on earth should he have done so, and kept so close and yet so far from Colossians?

If Paul did write the letter, where and when was it written, and for what reason? In the first place, the destination, to the Ephesians, is missing in some important manuscripts. Marcion, in the second century, had a copy addressed to Laodiceans. And it seems hardly credible that there should be no personal greetings to a city where Paul had spent three years of his life. The best explanation would seem to be that Paul sent a general letter to the churches in Asia Minor, and the copy that was included in the Pauline collection was addressed to Ephesus, although others were in existence.

The letter breathes a serene air. The great conflict in the Church between Jew and Gentile Christian has been resolved. 'Christ is himself our peace. Jew and Gentile, he has made the two one, and in his own body of flesh and blood he has broken down the enmity which stood like a dividing wall between them' (Ephesians 2:13ff). The theme of the Epistle is the risen and ascended Christ, and its vision is not merely of the Church, but of the whole cosmos brought into a unity in Christ (1:10). A great commentator sums up the Epistle as follows:

The circumcision question was dead. Other questions were being raised; and to these the Epistle to the Colossians in particular is controversially addressed. This done, his mind is free for one supreme exposition, non-controversial, positive, fundamental, of the great doctrine of his life – that doctrine into which he had been advancing year by year under the discipline of his unique circumstances – the doctrine of the unity of mankind in Christ and of the purpose of God for the world through the Church.[8]

In the letter he speaks of himself as 'a prisoner for the Lord's sake' (Ephesians 4:1). That suggests either Caesarea (where he was imprisoned after his arrest in the Temple at Jerusalem) or Rome (where he lived in his own hired house waiting for his appeal to be heard before Caesar). Another possibility is Ephesus (where he wrote that he had 'fought with wild beasts' (1 Corinthians 15:32); but even if Paul meant this literally, it is unlikely that he wrote a letter *from* Ephesus which now contains the words 'to Ephesus'. Many commentators assume Roman authorship, during a period when he looked back serenely on his former ministry. But a strong case can be made for Caesarea (A.D. 57–59), and the matter rests on the date of Colossians with which the Epistle is so closely connected.

THE EPISTLE TO THE PHILIPPIANS

Paul founded the church at Philippi during his second missionary journey, when he left the mainland of Asia at Troas, and crossed to this Roman colony. Paul preached on the Sabbath and a 'God-fearer' called Lydia responded to his message, and Paul stayed thenceforward in her house. Paul was accused of causing a disturbance after he had exorcised a slave-girl, thus depriving her owners of their source of income. He was taken before the magistrates and put into prison. His gaolers were converted and discovered that Paul was a Roman citizen, and escorted him out of the prison. The magistrates apologized to him before Paul went on his way.

From the number of personal greetings in the letter, Paul evidently kept in touch with the church at Philippi. He was in prison when he wrote this letter (Philippians 1:7,17). The Philippians had sent a contribution of money through Epaphroditus (2:25; 4:18). They had sent him similar presents before (4:15), but there had been little opportunity for so doing for some time. Epaphroditus had fallen dangerously ill while with Paul. Paul knew that the Philippians would be anxious about him, and therefore sent him back, together with this letter. The letter is written in a warm, affectionate tone. It not only contains his own heartfelt thanks, but also information about himself, about other matters of interest, together with such advice as the condition of the church (as Epaphroditus had told him) seemed to require. The letter contains an outburst against the Judaizers who were insisting that Gentile converts should be circumcized, which suggests that even at this point in his ministry, Paul was still capable of strong language and bitter feelings (3:2ff).

Once again the place of origin could be Ephesus, or Caesarea, or Rome. The last named has been most popular among biblical scholars. The matter is best settled by comparing the many allusions to individuals named in the Epistle with what is known of these people's movements in the Acts of the Apostles. An Ephesian authorship is not impossible, although it is odd that Acts is silent about a long and serious imprisonment of Paul there. But the references to the praetorian guard (Philippians 1:13) and to Caesar's household (4:22) seem to point rather to Caesarea or

Rome. Perhaps Caesarea is to be preferred, since Paul is known to have been imprisoned there, whereas at Rome he lived in his own hired house (Acts 28:30). The Epistle may therefore be dated some time between A.D. 57 and 59. It must be admitted however that an earlier date would better suit its affinity of style with the earlier letters of Paul.

THE EPISTLE TO THE COLOSSIANS

Colossae was a city situated on the river Lycus in Phrygia, not far from Laodicea. It was a wild region of picturesque beauty. Paul neither founded the church there, nor had he visited it when he wrote his Epistle. On his second missionary journey he went into the Phrygian region of the province of Galatia, but passed through Mysia, east of the Lycus valley. On his third missionary journey, he revisited the churches he had already founded. However, Paul had many contacts at Colossae, and it was within his region of care. He was sending Tychicus with this letter (as with the Epistle to the Ephesians), and in any case Onesimus was a native of Colossae, and Paul was sending him back also with the letter (Colossians 4:9).

Paul was writing because of the false teaching current at Colossae. The gnostic heresy which Paul was combating began from a sense of the distance of God from his creation: angelic beings were necessary to mediate between God and the world. Paul opposed this by his conviction that Christ spanned heaven and earth. In Christ the complete being of the Godhead dwells embodied (2:9). 'To their cosmical speculations and to their religious yearnings alike, Jesus Christ is the true answer.'[9] All things were created through him. Christ is the 'sole and absolute link between God and humanity. Nothing short of his personality would suffice as a medium of reconciliation.'[10] So Christ is the mediator of God in creation and in salvation.

The Colossian heresy affected matters of behaviour as much as belief. The heretics wanted to escape from impurity and to be immune from evil. They had associated the material world with evil; and so they fenced their life about with a code of prohibitions: 'Why let people dictate to you: Do not handle this, do not taste that, do not touch the other – all of them things that must perish as soon as they are used? This is to follow merely human injunctions and teaching' (2:20). Just as Paul borrowed their key term – *pleroma* (fullness) – to insist that all the fullness of deity dwelt in Christ, so here he borrows their belief that material things are evil in order to point out that if Christ is at the centre of their being, they have left behind wordly considerations – 'Then put to death those parts of you which belong to the earth – fornication, indecency, lust . . . then put on the garments which suit God's chosen people, his own, his beloved; compassion, kindness, humility . . .' (Colossians 3:5–12).

Paul was in prison when he wrote this 'captivity epistle', as he was when he wrote Ephesians and Philippians. The close connection with Ephesians suggests that it was written at the same time. We have discarded Ephesus as the place from which Ephesians was sent. In any case, the Christology of Colossians – 'his is the primacy over all created things' (1:15) – seems rather advanced for an early date in Paul's ministry. Onesimus accompanied Tychicus with the letter, and Timothy, Aristarchus and Luke are all mentioned in both Epistles. This suggests that Paul sent off the Epistle to the Colossians and the one to Philemon at the same time, by the same hand; and if so, Ephesus was rather close as a place of refuge for a runaway slave. This leaves either Caesarea or Rome as places of origin. Since Paul was in prison at Caesarea but under house arrest in Rome, the former suits better, especially as this place of origin fits well with the personal remarks at the end of the letter.

THE FIRST EPISTLE TO THE THESSALONIANS

This letter, far from coming near the close of Paul's ministry, is the first extant letter from his hand. Paul on his second missionary journey came to Thessalonika down the Via Egnatia from Philippi via Amphipolis and Apollonia. He was there for three Sabbaths, but a commotion was caused by Jewish objectors, and Paul had to leave under cover of darkness for Beroea (Acts 17:1–10). From there he made his way to Athens and thence to Corinth. Naturally Paul would have been concerned about the welfare of the infant church at Thessalonika, after such a start. While Paul was at Athens he despatched Timothy back to Thessalonika, because he 'could bear it no longer' (1 Thessalonians 3:1). Timothy rejoined Paul at Corinth, along with Silas (Acts 18:5 does not mention their being left behind at Beroea and their subsequent journey to Paul at Athens). Paul had gone on to Corinth by the time that they had returned from Thessalonika. The Epistle was written from Corinth, probably in A.D. 50, within a year of the founding of the church at Thessalonika.

The news that they brought necessitated this letter. It is hardly surprising that, with such short a period of instruction, the Thessalonian church suffered from 'shortcomings' (3:10) in the faith of its members. They were bothered about a matter on which Paul had had no opportunity of teaching them. Some Christians had died since Paul had left the city; and members of the congregation were concerned whether these would enjoy the same advantages on the Day of the Lord as survivors. They also needed encouragement about themselves. Paul had taught them that without blameless living they could not enter into the joy of the Lord at his coming. Would they then be excluded? Paul explains these matters in a way that should have set their minds at rest. He needed not only to put them right in their faith, but also in their behaviour. Perhaps not surprisingly in those who had only lately been converted from paganism, the Thessalonians needed reminding about God's demand for sexual purity, and his calling to holiness. Paul gives this teaching together with a generous and warm expression of gratitude for the Thessalonians' courageous faith and their loving response to their new-found Gospel – 'a model for all believers in Macedonia and Achaia' (1:8). Evidently opposition to the young church had continued after Paul's departure.

THE SECOND EPISTLE TO THE THESSALONIANS

Paul's letter did not have quite the instant effect for which he had hoped. He had felt it necessary to defend himself from attacks in the first letter (1 Thessalonians 2:10). These suspicions seem to have been allayed. Paul does not find it necessary to write any further on sexual morality for the 'weak'. But the story had got about in some way – Paul is not clear quite how – that Paul had said that the Day of the Lord had already arrived. He makes it clear that before that could happen certain events would precede it, and they had not yet taken place. The result of this misunderstanding is that some Thessalonian Christians had downed tools and had stopped working. Paul renews his dictum 'the man who will not work shall not eat', and encourages the members of the church to get on quietly with their own work and to mind their own business.

There are those who think that this second letter is a forgery. Arguments are derived from its language and style, from its relationship to 1 Thessalonians, and from the character of its doctrinal contents. Some words are alleged to be un-Pauline, and 2 Thessalonians is said to be too close to 1 Thessalonians to be written by the same person. (But why then is it not too close for a fabricator to have written it?) Again it is said that whereas in 1 Thessalonians Paul teaches that the Last Day is close at hand, in 2 Thessalonians he teaches that certain events must precede it. Indeed it is asked whether Paul himself could have held a view which required apocalyptic signs before the coming of Christ. Various suggestions have been made to account for these differences: that one Epistle was written to the Gentile church, the other to the Jewish church at Thessalonika, that Timothy wrote one of the letters, that there is an interpolation into the text of 2 Thessalonians, or that 2 Thessalonians is a second-century forgery. All of these hypotheses show the subjectiveness of such arguments. Who is to say what words Paul could or could not use? Why is Paul expected always to be consistent? Why is he not allowed to repeat himself? It is usually simpler to imagine Paul writing a disputed letter than to imagine credible circumstances in which another writer could have written a letter which bears his name.

THE FIRST AND SECOND EPISTLES TO TIMOTHY AND THE EPISTLE TO TITUS

It has been part of received critical orthodoxy until a few years ago that the so-called Pastoral Epistles (1 and 2 Timothy and Titus) are not genuine letters from the hand of Paul. They are said to be written in a style which is not Pauline (including the quotation of Christian hymns); they are said to show ecclesiastical interests which were not Paul's; they are alleged to use non-Pauline language; and they are thought to reveal a doctrinal attitude which is Paulinist, but which belongs to a post-Pauline age, when the Church needed consolidation, and when Pauline thought had lost its inspiration. Most scholars held that all the letters were concocted in Paul's name in the second century in order to keep the churches which Paul had founded in the purity of Pauline belief and practice.

A difficulty arose, because these Epistles (and in particular 1 Timothy) contain allusions which it is very hard to imagine anyone making up. Why should anyone declare that Paul had consigned Hymenaeus and Alexander to Satan, had he not done so (1 Timothy 1:20)? Why should a forger have concocted that story of Paul leaving behind his cloak at Troas (2 Timothy 4:13)? And so the theory of composition was amended so that the present Epistles were thought to have been built up around some genuine Pauline fragments which had been, for some unknown reason, mysteriously preserved, and which contained personal remarks and greetings. This theory seems even less credible than that of outright fabrication. Some have therefore suggested that the differences from the other Paulines are due to Paul's use of a secretary. But so he did for his other letters. Today the view is gaining ground that they are genuinely Pauline, and show a pastoral concern of the Apostle very different from what is found elsewhere. It could be that different circumstances produce a very different style and vocabulary and method of approach.

The First Epistle to Timothy is concerned with church order. There is instruction on Christian prayer and on the requirements for Christian leadership. There is a call not to fall into false teaching. There are instructions concerning the official recognition of widows, who are the proper responsibility of the Church; and also concerning elders; and there are personal exhortations to Timothy. If Paul wrote the letter, when and where? Because of the differences between these letters and the other extant Pauline letters, they have often been attributed to a very late stage of the Apostle's ministry, after his release from Rome on successful appeal to the Emperor and before he met his martyrdom. Since no one knows anything about such a period, any such reconstruction cannot be denied. Can any other period be suggested? It has been said (not very convincingly) that they were written during Paul's custody in Rome. Another suggestion is that 1 Timothy was written from Troas in A.D. 55, that Titus was written in A.D. 57 when Paul was en route from Miletus to Jerusalem, and that 2 Timothy was sent from Caesarea in A.D. 58. These dates and places are surmises, and no certainty can be attained.

The second letter to Timothy contains far more personal allusions than the First Epistle. It concentrates on the character of a Christian minister. It is much shorter than the First Epistle. The Epistle to Titus is shorter still, and contains instruction about training for the Christian life. These three Epistles are written to Paul's chief aides in his great missionary work. They seem curiously unintimate for letters addressed to those who were closest to Paul in his apostolic labours. But perhaps they were intended to be read not only by Timothy and Titus but also in public to those associated with them in their missionary labours. In any case, we must not confuse the standards of this age with those of Paul's.

THE EPISTLE TO PHILEMON

This is the only purely private letter in the Pauline corpus. Philemon had a runaway slave, Onesimus, who had escaped to the city where Paul was imprisoned, and who had attached himself to Paul, and had become a

Christian. Paul sent the slave back to his master with a letter asking him to give Onesimus a welcome. He would have preferred to keep Onesimus by him, but felt constrained to return him. Paul promises to pay for any wrong that Onesimus may have done Philemon by running away, and for any money he may have taken. He recollects that Philemon owes his very self to Paul, and he is confident that Philemon will respond. It is a good letter, and any Christian would surely feel proud to have penned such a missive. Timothy, Demas, Epaphras, Luke and Archipius are all mentioned, both in this letter and in the letter to the Colossians. This suggests that both letters were taken together to Colossae. The Epistle to Philemon should be therefore dated from Caesarea around A.D. 57. It gives us a touching insight into the pastoral care and love which Paul showed for individuals. The great Apostle to the Gentiles not only took thought for the grand missionary strategy: the fate of a runaway slave was very dear indeed to his heart.

4 PAUL THE THEOLOGIAN

In this chapter I am going to give a systematic account of Paul's thinking. To a certain extent this is an artificial construction. Paul never imagined, when he dictated his letters, that people would go through them with a fine tooth comb, noting for example all the times that he used a certain word, and comparing what he had said in one letter with what he had said in another, taking a bit from here and a bit from there in order to give a connected account of his thinking. Few sets of letters – say, a series of pastoral letters from a bishop – could stand up to that kind of treatment. Views change: words are used now with one nuance, now with another: what we say is often adapted to the peculiar circumstances to which our words are addressed. None the less it is possible to give a more or less systematic account of Paul's thinking, providing its limitations are realized. In so doing, the most systematic of his extant writings, the Epistle to the Romans, is particularly useful.

We shall not begin by considering Paul's debt to Greek or Rabbinic thought:[1] we begin with what he wrote.[2] It might seem at first sight that we should start with Paul's thinking about Christ. That is certainly where he began. According to Paul, God sent his Son, who died as a sacrifice for sin. God raised him from the dead, and sent the Spirit of his Son into our hearts. Thereby he saved us from the power of sin, death, and the evil powers, liberating us from the Law with its impossible commandments, and freeing us to live after the law of Love. However, even this brief summary assumes a background of thought about sin and death so strange to the twentieth century, that we must go back to them in order to begin.[3]

We tend to mean by sin an act of transgression. That was not what it meant to Paul.[4] For him sin is an evil power which has insinuated itself into the lower side of human nature. Sin is alive and lives in a man (Romans 7:17). A man, under the dominion of sin, becomes its slave (Romans 6:17). Freeing a man from sin is like liberating him from the rule of a tyrant (Romans 6:22). For Paul the rule of sin is universal. As a first-century Jew he took the story of the fall of Adam in Genesis as a historical fact. And so 'by one man sin entered the world' (Romans 5:12). He does not explain how sin passed from Adam to all who came after him. He is content simply to state it as a fact, confirmed by experience.

Sin is intimately connected with law. Sin involves rebelliousness against God. Instead of being grateful and obedient creatures giving thanks to their Creator, men have become his disgruntled, disaffected and disobedient enemies. This interior rebelliousness becomes apparent through transgressing the law. Without law sin as it were remains dormant and quiescent. It is stimulated to virulence by the advent of law. 'Until the law sin was in the world: but sin is not imputed where there is no law' (Romans 5:13). When sin is made manifest by transgression it becomes visible and actionable, because there is a deliberate refusal to carry out a commandment of God.

Paul sees the Law of Moses having just this effect. As a good Jew Paul could not possibly bring himself to say that the Law is evil. It was 'holy, just and good' (Romans 7:12), even 'spiritual' (Romans 7:14). 'Is the Law sin?' he asks, and then recoils from the blasphemy of what he has said – 'God forbid', he answers. The Law, however good in itself, is wholly bad in its effects. The Law gave sin its chance. In an autobiographical sketch, Paul says:

'I was alive without the Law once' – referring to his childhood – 'but when the commandment came, sin revived, and I died' (Romans 7:9).

The experience of Paul is the experience of every man, Jew and Gentile. The Law in its entirety was binding upon every Jew (Galatians 5:3). But it is impossible to keep the whole Law. The slightest transgression incurs guilt; and the feeling of achievement brought about by a successful keeping of the Law induces just that attitude of self-satisfaction and self-reliance which is clean contrary to the Law. The Jew has to live under the Law, and yet 'all who rely on the works of the law are under a curse' (Galatians 3:10).

Gentiles are in no better case. Although they do not have to keep the Law of Moses, they have the law of God, the natural law; and they break this. Paul was speaking to a pagan world that was essentially religious. He acknowledged that pagans believed in God; but they refused to give God his due: worship, obedience and reverence.

And so all mankind is in the grip of sin, an evil which infests and infects humanity. It is a kind of evil power. In the world of Paul's day there was a common belief in demons. The Jews in particular thought of the fallen angels as infesting the world and causing men to sin. We shall not understand the extraordinary phenomenon of primitive Christianity unless we realize that it brought liberation from the cruel bondage of these evil powers. They are variously described as 'the rulers of this age' who crucified the Lord of glory (1 Corinthians 2:6), the elemental spirits (Galatians 4:9) or 'principalities and powers, the world rulers of this present darkness, spiritual wickedness in high places' (Ephesians 6:15).

The result of man's bondage to sin and his enslavement to the evil powers is that he is alienated from God. Instead of being God's loving child, he has become his enemy. He lives under the Wrath.[5] This wrath of God is manifested in various ways. Man has a bad conscience, a realization that he has transgressed the limits fixed by God. Wars, destruction, cataclysms, disasters are also manifestations of the Wrath. Man's life is subjectively painful and objectively disastrous. And when God brings to an end this world order – and Paul in his earlier letters did not think that it could be long delayed – men will face judgement, and the verdict will be damnation; eternal alienation from God and suffering. Men will be faced with final death. Already sin has resulted in death entering the world. 'As sin came into the world through one man, and death through sin, so death spread to all men because all men sinned' (Romans 5:12). The wages of sin is death. Paul meant by death more than physical dissolution. It represented spiritual extinction as much as bodily corruption. Death is the end-term of that process which is the result of sin.

Death is the final outcome of what Paul called 'life after the flesh'. We tend to think of this as meaning a sensual way of life. That was not primarily Paul's meaning. Of course he used flesh in different senses (as he also used death); but 'living after the flesh' can perhaps best be rendered as *materialism*. A man who is alienated from God puts his trust not in God but in himself. He lives not by the grace of God, but purely by his own efforts. He boasts about his own achievements. Flesh for Paul means characteristically man in his distance and separation from God, resulting in weakness and infirmity. Because this shows itself in man's outward behaviour, Paul expresses this by the word 'flesh'. But to 'live after the flesh' does not mean to lead a life that is prey to all the physical passions. It includes this meaning, but primarily it means to live apart from God in the fallible power of one's own strength. Of course there is a sense in which no one can help living in the flesh. We are creatures of flesh and blood. It is part of the physical order that this should be so. Paul knows and believes that there is nothing wrong with the physical ties of sex or race as such. It is only when a man lives his life apart from God that these become instruments of sin.

All men live in the flesh. It is the common condition of humanity. We are bound together in the solidarity of creation.[6] Paul sees all mankind as bound together in the solidarity of fallen creation. Paul, by his reference to Adam, shows that for him sin is universal and infests all human relationships. Paul can use 'flesh' not merely to designate particular men, but humanity bound together in solidarity against God. And so to live after the flesh is to live under sin. Because of his sinful condition man is condemned to live after the flesh. Here then is the human predicament as Paul sees it. Man is under the power of sin, condemned to live after the flesh, subject to corruption, subject to the law and yet condemned by the law. He can do absolutely nothing to help himself. His position is hopeless. Paul is sensitive to the suggestion that this analysis does not show up God in a very good light. If the Law inevitably brought sin, why did God give men the Law? If all men are destined to death, how does this show the righteousness and the goodness of God? Some of the answers that Paul gives to these questions are not very satisfactory; but then no one has ever answered them all satisfactorily. However, to the question about the Law, Paul replied that it was only an interim measure. It was never intended by God as the permanent condition of human existence. It was a *paidagogus*, the slave who took a minor to school, a custodian until Christ comes (Galatians 3:24). Incidentally, what a brave and daring image to use! Paul wrote: 'Before faith came, we were confined under the law, kept under restraint until faith shall be revealed' Galatians 3:23). Law brought to a head the evil of sin, as a poultice draws out the poison before a boil can be lanced. The Law was given 'in order that sin might be shown to be sin, and through the commandment might be become sinful beyond measure' (Romans 7:13). God had to show up the situation in its true colours before he could take steps to put it right.

God sent his Son.[7] Paul does not analyse exactly what he means by the Son. He seems to mean a pre-existent being, 'The divine nature was his from the first; yet he did not think to snatch at equality with God, but made himself nothing, assuming the nature of a slave. Bearing the human likeness, revealed in human shape, he humbled himself. . .' (Philippians 2:6f).[8] More than angelic status is intended, for the Son is the agent of all creation (1 Corinthians 8:6; Colossians 1:16f), a concept which approximates in some respect to Stoic teaching about the Logos. In another passage Paul writes (Romans 11:36) that all things are through God (not through Christ), a passage which shows something of the fluidity of Paul's thinking, and the extent to which he equated Christ, if not with God, at least with the functions of God. But who of us would like to be taken to task for our lack of clarity in speaking about the different functions of the three members of the Blessed Trinity, and that (so far as we are concerned) after, not before, that doctrine has been defined?

God sent his Son. Christ identified himself completely with the human situation without being contaminated by it. Instead he transformed it. 'God has done what the law, weakened by the flesh, could not do: sending his own Son in the likeness of sinful flesh and for sin, he condemned sin in the flesh' (Romans 8:3). Christ, far from committing sin, 'died out' on sin (Romans 6:10). And so he passed beyond its power, for sin could only gain entrance through the flesh and when Jesus died he put off the flesh. And by his death Christ showed that sin had over-reached itself. Since Christ had not sinned, he did not deserve to die; but in as much as he did die, God thereby pronounced as it were a judgement of 'guilty' upon sin. And so Christ was victorious over sin, and won his Father's vindication.

We share Christ's victory over sin because we are identified with Christ. This is what it means to be 'in Christ'. 'We are dead to sin', cries Paul triumphantly (Romans 6:2). After death sin can have no further hold over a man, so that if we die with Christ, we are freed from sin. 'We know that our old self was crucified with him, so that the sinful body might be destroyed, and we might no longer be enslaved to sin' (Romans 6:6). Those who belong to Christ have crucified the flesh with its passions and desires (Galatians 5:24).

What Paul writes about sin can be parallelled by what he writes about death. Death is universal. Christ identified with men completely, so that he too suffered death. 'He became obedient unto death, even the death upon the Cross' (Philippians 2:8). By the very fact of his death, he passed beyond its power. It has no further dominion over him. And so when his Father raised him from the dead, he was victorious over death and all the evil powers: he was given a name that is above every name (Philippians 2:9). He made a show of the powers and principalities upon the Cross (Colossians 2:15). Christ's achievements are shared by all who are identified with him. Those who belong to Christ have been freed by Christ from the 'elemental spirits' of the world (Galatians 4:3f). Christians have stripped off their old self (Ephesians 4:22), just as Christ stripped off his old self on the Cross (Colossians 2:15). They are planted together with Christ in his death (Romans 6:5), crucified with him (Romans 6:6); buried with him (Romans 6:3).

Just as Christ identified himself with flesh, sin and death, so also he identified himself with men under the law. He was born of a woman, born under the law (Galatians 4:4). He even became a curse for us (Galatians

3:13). This does not mean that Jesus was actually accursed, but that he suffered the effect of the curse, thus drawing its sting. As a result of this, Christ died; and thereafter the law could have no further power over him, for the law only has jurisdiction over a man so long as he is alive. So Christ, by 'dying out' on the law passed beyond its power too. Similarly all who are identified with Christ have also passed beyond the law's power. 'Christ abolished in his flesh the law of commandments and ordinances' (Ephesians 2:15). 'He cancelled the bond that stood against us with its legal demands; this he set aside, nailing it to the Cross' (Colossians 2:14). As a result the believer also 'is dead to the law through the body of Christ' (Romans 7:4). In fact Paul uses several arguments to show that Christ has broken the power of the Law; and it must be admitted that some of these are better than others! But his main point stands.

Paul asserts that this great victory of Christ, in which Christians share by being identified with him, fulfils the promises of God. These promises had first been given to Abraham years before the Law had ever been given. And so the promises were given to Abraham not because of his submission to the Law – it was not yet there to submit to – but because of his faith.

Paul uses many images and metaphors to describe this great victory of Christ which won freedom for all men. It must be admitted that when stressing its objective nature he seems to assume that the victory is assured for all: in other passages, when he is emphasizing that no one can earn or deserve a share in this victory, he speaks as though it can only be appropriated through faith. None the less the same images to describe it are used, whichever point he is emphasizing.

Sacrifice is an image rather remote from us today.[9] When Paul wrote, there were countless sacrifices made in the pagan temples of the Roman world, and every day the smoke of many sacrifices from the Jewish Temple rose over the city of Jerusalem. The image was one of the most common that he could have used. Paul has many different types of sacrifice by which to describe Christ's death. It is a Passover sacrifice, an expiatory sacrifice, a sin offering, an offering of a sweet savour. It was the sacrifice of the Suffering Servant foretold by Isaiah. Sacrifice in the Old Testament was the appointed means by which God brought men back into relationship with himself. It was an image of cost. It produced an objective result. It signified release of life. All these ideas underlay the imagery which Paul used. Paul did not attempt to *explain* Christ's death by the Old Testament sacrifices; but he made use of them as imagery which helped his hearers to understand its true significance.

Paul also used the imagery of redemption. Nowadays the word is perhaps most associated with the Stock Exchange – the buying back of stocks and shares by those who issued them. Buying back is the root meaning. It was used in the ancient world in connection with the liberation of slaves.[10] On payment of a sum of money a slave was freed from his master and placed under the protection of a god. Again, redemption is an image of cost, an image of liberation, and it was an objective act. And so 'you have been bought with a price' (1 Corinthians 6:20); 'With freedom did Christ set us free' (Galatians 5:1). Once we had been slaves to sin. But through Christ's redemption we have been freed from slavery and adopted back as the children of God. 'We have received the spirit of adoption whereby we cry Abbah, Father.' We are all sons of God through faith (Galatians 3:26).

Occasionally Paul uses the more personal image of reconciliation. God 'was in Christ reconciling the world to himself' (2 Corinthians 5:19). 'While we were yet sinners Christ died for us and that is God's own proof of his love for us' (Romans 5:8). Here God himself takes the initiative. A person who has caused a rift is powerless to make a reconciliation. It must be the injured party who takes the initiative. God has done that through Christ. This is the most personal image that Paul uses, perhaps the most profound.

He preferred however most of all the image of the lawcourt. This is probably because Paul was so concerned about the relationship between the Law and the Gospel. Through Christ God has justified sinners. This statement does not mean that God has made men righteous. A man cannot have his character altered, as it were by a flick of a switch. On the other hand justification does not mean that God has accounted us righteous, although we are in fact unrighteous. That would imply a legal fiction, which would be unworthy of God. Justification means that God has acted to put mankind in a right relationship to himself. He has come to our aid, vindicated us, set us right with himself.[11] We are therefore acquitted through no effort of our own. Paul's chief aim in using this imagery is to show that man's salvation is due entirely to God, and in no way depends on human achievements. 'It is God who justifies', he says (Romans 8:33). 'We are justified freely by his grace' (Romans 3:23). Justification is grounded in the death of Christ (Romans 3:25). We all deserve condemnation. But God has not dealt with us like a righteous judge: he has acted as a loving father. Paul never says that Jesus died *instead of* us: he does not take our place, as it were, in the firing line. He died *on behalf of* us. As we have seen, Jesus did not deserve to die; and by his death God passed judgement on sin. The death of Jesus therefore shows God's righteous nature: it shows also the seriousness of sin. The Cross makes clear God's condemnation of sin as much as his acceptance of sinners.

The death of Jesus is universal in its efficacy. It reverses the sin of Adam; and in this sense Jesus can be called 'the Second Adam'. 'As one man's trespass led to condemnation for all men, so one man's act of righteousness leads to acquittal and life for all men' (Romans 5:18). Although Christ's death is universal in efficacy, it needs faith for its benefits to be appropriated by each person.

What does faith mean here? It is a word in Pauline usage with many overtones. There is what Bultmann has called a 'structure of faith'. Abraham for Paul is the greatest example of a man of faith. He believed in the promises of God even when circumstances were right against him. God had promised him that he would become the father of a great nation, at a time when his wife was well past the age of child-bearing. How could it come to pass that in him all the nations of the earth would be blessed? Yet Abraham put all his faith on the promises of God, and believed – and for this reason Abraham was 'justified by faith'. But caution here is needed. His justification was not due to his faith: it was the free and undeserved gift of God. Faith was the means by which Abraham appropriated this great promise of God.

Christians of course are in a somewhat different situation. Abraham only had a promise. Christians have not a mere promise on which to rely, but a promise and its fulfilment in the work of God in Christ. That is the concrete ground of their faith. Faith is the opposite of boasting. It means casting oneself on God rather than relying on one's own powers (Romans 3:27). 'Works' imply self-sufficiency: faith implies that our sufficiency is of God. Faith has nothing to do with circumcision, because that belongs to the Law, and Abraham believed the promise of God not after but before he was circumcised. Faith on the part of man is the correlative of grace on the part of God. A man's faith enables him to accept what God in his kindness gives regardless of his merits.

This is the key meaning of faith for Paul. But the concept as a whole is very rich.[12] It has an intellectual content ('believing that'). It implies obedience towards God. Paul is not very interested in the psychological aspect of faith. For him faith is an attitude of the whole personality rather than a sensation of the soul or a disposition of the feelings. It belongs more to the sphere of will than of the affections. Because it concerns the whole man, faith includes both verbal articulation (Romans 10:9) and practical expression (Colossians 1:10).

Faith is the correlative of grace. Paul uses the latter word with a special and personal meaning.[13] For him it means either the free gift of God, or the attitude of benevolence and beneficence which issues in man's close and personal relationship with God. Paul does not say much above the love *of God*. He says more about *our* loving response to the Gospel. If hope is the form of faith projected into the future, love is its present expression. In speaking about *God*, Paul prefers to speak of the grace of God. For Paul the Incarnation is the supreme act of grace: 'the grace of God and the free gift in the grace of that one man Jesus Christ abounded for many' (Romans 5:15).

What does Paul think of 'this one man Jesus Christ'? He was clear that Jesus shared to the full our human nature (Romans 8:3). Jesus was born of a woman, born under the law (Galatians 4:4), on the human level born of the stock of David (Romans 1:3). For Paul Jesus also had a divine nature. Like the rest of the early Church, he believed that Jesus was the Christ (although for him this had more or less become a proper name rather than a descriptive term). Jesus was also Lord, to be worshipped and adored. Jesus did not originate on earth. He was pre-existent, as has been discussed earlier. (Whether Paul got this concept from Judaism or Hellenistic religions is much debated). His divine nature was not manifested during his life or his death – apart from the act of dying Paul in his·extant letters seems almost indifferent to the events of Jesus's life. The divine nature of the Son of God was disclosed at his Resurrection. 'On the level of the spirit – the Holy Spirit – he was declared Son of God by a mighty act in that he rose from the dead' (Romans 1:4). His Resurrection was no mere resuscitation. 'God raised him to the heights and bestowed on him the name above all names, that at the name of Jesus every knee should bow – in heaven, on earth and in the depths – and every tongue confess that Jesus Christ is Lord, to the glory of God the Father' (Philippians 2:9ff).

Although Paul was clear that Jesus was divine, he did not equate him with God. God is 'the Father of our Lord Jesus Christ'. Christ is clearly subordinate to the Father, and in the end he will hand over the Kingdom to God the Father (1 Corinthians 15:24). None the less although Christ is not equated with God, he has the function of God. Paul can speak indifferently of the grace of God and the grace of Christ, he can write 'if God wills' or 'if Christ wills'; he mentions the judgement of God and the judgement of Christ. He can call himself the servant of God or the servant of Christ. He can speak of creation through God or through Christ. Of course Paul did not work out the Doctrine of the Trinity any more than he worked out the Doctrine of the Incarnation. None the less we find in his writings an unconscious grasp of both these doctrines *in nuce*.

When Jesus ascended into the heavens, God, according to Paul, 'put all things under his feet and made him the head over all things for the Church, which is his body, the fullness of him who fills all in all' (Ephesians 1:22). According to Paul Christ has several bodies. He had a human body which was crucified on the Cross. He was raised to the heavenly places in a spiritual body, not the old body of flesh and blood which cannot inherit the Kingdom of Heaven (1 Corinthians 15:50). His body is the mode of existence by which Christ is seen to be alive and through which he lives. A body is not to be equated with a person. A person lives through his body but is not absolutely limited by it. In the same way, Christ's life is not limited by the bodies through which he lives.

Into this spiritual body Christians are incorporated through faith by baptism. They are members of Christ's body and so they are members of the Church. They actually belong to Christ: they are part of Christ: they are membranes of Christ.[14] In typical Pauline language they are 'in Christ'. Sometimes this phrase is used by Paul in a loose sense, almost designating a Christian environment; but most typically it means belonging to Christ, being part of him, being a member of his body.[15]

To be 'in Christ' is the same as being 'in the Spirit'. The Spirit cannot be fully identified with the ascended and risen Lord, because the Spirit is poured out on earth, while the ascended Lord is in the heavenly places at the right hand of God. But the Spirit is not, as in the Lucan writings, the substitute for Christ. On the contrary the Spirit is the Spirit of Christ. It fills the Church, and makes it become the body of Christ. The Spirit manifests itself in many gifts, and its effects are seen in the many fruits of the Spirit. While different individuals have particular gifts of the Spirit, the Spirit itself is the inheritance of the whole Church. Christians only share in the Spirit because they are members of the Church. This participation in the Spirit brings freedom and liberty, because it is incorporated into the life of Christ.

And so Paul contrasts the Spirit with the Law, because the Spirit brings freedom while the Law brings bondage. Paul also contrasts the Spirit with the Flesh. 'Living after the Spirit' means living in the power of God, while 'living after the flesh' means living in the fallible power of one's own strength. The Spirit manifests itself in power, and through it mighty acts are done. It confers upon men the status of sonship. It is holy, because the Spirit comes from God and sets apart the Church for God. The Spirit is not in Pauline thinking an impersonal force. He works personally in the Church and in men, because the Spirit is the Spirit of Jesus. As Christ prays for his disciples, so the Spirit makes intercession for us: he helps us to pray because he is the Spirit of Christ.[16]

Men and women receive the Spirit through Baptism. (Whether their children were also baptized is another – disputed – matter.) Baptism is the appointed means of entry into the Church. It is the way by which a person becomes a part of Christ. It is the moment when a person is adopted into sonship with God. It is a death to the old life and a start to the new. It is recreation and rebirth. At the heart of Paul's thinking is the death and resurrection of Christ. This is the central mystery of his faith. Baptism is the sacramental means of sharing in his death and rising with Christ in newness of life. As Christ died to the world in baptism, so Christians die to their old self, and share in the joy of the risen and ascended Lord. So baptism is once for all, for it commemorates and re-enacts in the individual the once for all work of Christ for mankind. It is much more than circumcision. The latter is merely an outward sign, but baptism is a kind of spiritual circumcision. It 'effects what it signifies' in the believer. Of course baptism can only be received with faith. It means identification with Christ. The old life is stripped off, rather like a suit of clothes. It is a kind of sealing – the mode through which God's people are marked out as Christ's. It is an anointing, because it is the occasion when the Holy Spirit is poured out on an individual. It is the start of the Christian life, the mark of our faith and the ground of our unity. 'By one Spirit we were all baptized into one body – Jews or Greeks, slaves or free – and all were made to drink of one Spirit' (1 Corinthians 12:13).[17] The life of the baptized is clearly marked out from paganism. The Church is the temple of the Holy Spirit, and so also is each individual Christian. Within the body the divine love of *agape* is active. The Christian is to lead a new life, pleasing to God, because he is a new creature. Christian ethics depend on the aorist past tense. God *has* reconciled us to himself: *therefore* we are to act in a Christlike manner. 'Were you not raised with Christ? Then aspire to the realm above, where Christ is, seated on the right hand of God, and let your thoughts dwell on that higher realm, not on this earthly life . . . Then put to death those parts of you which belong to the earth – fornication, indecency, lust, foul cravings and the ruthless greed which is nothing less than idolatry . . . Now you must lay aside all anger, passion, malice, cursing, filthy talk . . .' (Colossians 3:1ff). For Paul Christian ethics could be summed up in the phrase 'Become what you are' (although he himself never put it like that). 'Act out your new status before God. Show yourselves in your true nature.'[18]

In the light of this we can understand Paul's ethical injunctions. The people of the new churches which he had founded had been accustomed to very different standards of behaviour in their pre-Christian days. Paul often has occasion to recall them to their new way of life. All that they do must be 'in the Lord', Whether it concerns their relationship to their masters (in the case of slaves) or family life, or Christian fellowship. The injunctions themselves, in the form of house-codes, do not differ greatly from Stoic ethical injunctions of the time; but the spirit is quite different.[19] Christians are to be holy, for they belong to God who is holy and righteous, and they are filled with the Holy Spirit of God. They are to be obedient to God, as Christ obeyed his Father. They are to be thankful. They are no longer to be bound by the Jewish Law, for Christ is the fulfilling of the Law. But they must show forbearance for those who are weak, and who still feel bound to obey the Law's injunctions. The keynote of all their attitudes and all their actions is to be love. 'Above all these things put on love, which binds everything together in perfect harmony' (Colossians 3:14). Paul's inmost convictions above love are set out in inimitable words in 1 Corinthians 13.

Paul's letters are addressed to individual churches; and so it is natural that he should express his ideas about the nature of the Church.[20] His understanding of the Church as the body of Christ has already been noted, although it must be recognized that he sometimes uses the phrase to describe a church congregation, and sometimes to denote the universal Church of God. He also employs the imagery of marriage, in thinking of the Church as the bride of Christ (Ephesians 5:25–33; cf. 2 Corinthians 11:2). This was apt, because it denoted for him the permanence of the union between Christ and the Church, and the subordination of the latter to the former. Marriage is an institution which creates a close personal union in love between two persons who none the less remain distinct. The analogy holds good for the relationship between Christ and his Church. Paul sometimes uses a less personal image, that of a building. The Church is the house of God (1 Corinthians 3:9), the temple of God (2 Corinthians 6:16), a building which grows and increases and builds itself up in love (Ephesians 2:20–22). All these images are corporate. A man cannot in Paul's thinking be simply an individual Christian. A person is a Christian by belonging to the Church. There are various different congregations – the church at Corinth, and at Rome, at Colossae, and so on. These are local manifestations of the one universal church of God.

The act of worship which represents the Church's relationship to Christ is the Eucharist, the means appointed by Christ for re-enacting the Church's unity and nature. It was no optional extra for Paul, but the gathering of the People of God (1 Corinthians 11:17ff).

By breaking bread together and sharing in the common cup, they participate anew in the body of Christ. By partaking of the one loaf they become what they are, one body (1 Corinthians 10:17). By eating the consecrated bread and drinking the consecrated wine, the Church of God 'proclaims Christ's death until he comes' (1 Corinthians 11:26). As in baptism individuals are brought into the Church and initiated into the death and resurrection of Christ, so in the Eucharist, as members of the Church, they share sacramentally in the death and resurrection of Christ, and renew their relationship with him. Baptism is the sacrament of initiation, and the Eucharist is the sacrament of continuation.

'Until he comes' – what did Paul believe about the end of the world? We tend to think of history going on and on, beginning with the evolution of species and continuing in cultural development. Paul however had a quite different view of history, in common with his age. The Jews thought of history coming to a decisive end. This 'aeon' would end, and the present world order would be wound up; and God would establish his Kingdom. In the first century A.D. there was a very general conviction among the Jews that this final crisis could not be long delayed.

Paul shared this conviction. Christ's advent meant that the Last Things had already been set in motion (1 Corinthians 10:11). The old aeon was already in process of passing away. Christ had already inaugurated the new aeon. Christians were living between the times of Christ's coming and the end of the aeon. To this extent theirs was an interim existence. Christ himself had already passed fully into the new aeon. His resurrection is the first fruits of the general resurrection (1 Corinthians 15:20). But clearly the new era had not yet fully come. The world, if no longer in the grip of evil powers, at least had not yet completely been freed from their influence.[21] To use an analogy common to the time when I began to study theology, D Day had taken place, victory was assured, but V Day had not yet been celebrated. There was therefore an interim quality about what Christ had done. It was effective, but not yet complete; but its very efficacy was a guarantee of its coming fulfilment. In particular the Holy Spirit was the seal of this Christian inheritance.

Men had been redeemed by Christ, but they still await the full redemption of their bodies. They had been justified; but they still await the time when they must stand before the judgement seat of Christ. They are in a state of salvation – and yet salvation still remains for the future. (There is a perceptive story of Bishop Westcott, once accosted by an Evangelist in a railway coach, who asked him 'Are you saved?' 'Do you mean *sesosmenos, sozomenos* or *sothesomenos*?' replied the Bishop, using the Greek words which Paul used to signify 'having been saved', 'in a state of salvation' and 'awaiting salvation'.) In this interim state, Christians live by faith, seeing as yet only in a glass darkly. When the perfect comes, that which is partial will pass away (1 Corinthians 13:9). Now Christians live by faith: soon they will live in glory. Already they were 'spiritual' because they had been given the Spirit;[22] but they still awaited a body that was spiritual. In this interim state they are to look not to the things that are transitory but to the things that are eternal.

This is the background of thought against which Paul's thinking must be understood – and also the thinking of most New Testament writers.[23] Paul believed that Christ would re-appear at the Last Day and gather his saints to himself. He does not say much about what life would be like thereafter, because he did not know. As we have noted earlier his perspective alters about the imminence of the Last Day, his sense of urgency fades, and he becomes world-affirming where earlier he had been world-denying. Whereas in the

Epistles to the Thessalonians the Last Day is an imminent cataclysmic event which reverses the present world order and vindicates the people of God, in the Epistle to the Ephesians there is no mention of the Advent of Christ, and the Last Day is seen more as the end of a process in which the Church has been building itself up under God, 'until we all attain to the unity of the faith and of the knowledge of the Son of God, to mature manhood, to the measure of the stature of the fullness of Christ' (Ephesians 4:13).

I have summarized here in short compass the main thinking of Paul, as we have it in his extant letters. I must end with the same warning with which I began. Paul did not think systematically, and to reconstruct his theology in this way is to give a false impression. The meaning of a sentence in a letter from the hand of Paul needs to be primarily understood within the context of that letter rather than as a collocation of words which form pieces of a vast jigsaw puzzle which when fitted together produce something which can be called 'Pauline theology'.[24] Words are used with a different nuance in different contexts, and in any case, as we have seen, Paul's own views can develop and change. Letters must not be seen as a formal statement of a considered dogmatic theology. However, despite these warnings, it is useful to see Paul's thinking as a whole, so far as this is possible. His was certainly an enormously impressive achievement. As we have seen, Paul did not consider that he was innovating, but drawing up and articulating the tradition which was common to the whole Church. The question arises as to what extent we can accept this thinking today in a very different age. To this we turn in the final chapter.

5 PAUL FOR TODAY

One of the most popular works of scholarship on Paul, bearing the title *The Meaning of Paul for Today*, is concerned only with what Paul said and meant. It contains no chapter on translating Paul's thought into today's concepts. The only concession that the author will make to the twentieth century is that he will write 'in modern terms'. The book was written by Professor C. H. Dodd. In an Introduction to a popular edition in 1958, nearly forty years after the book had first been published, he explained himself as follows:

> My main concern has been to bring out what I conceive to be the permanent significance of the Apostle's thought, in modern terms, and in relation to the general interests which occupy the mind of our generation. I find here a religious philosophy oriented throughout to the idea of a society or commonwealth of God. Such a philosophy finds ready contact with the dominant concerns of our own day. [1]

Those words belong to the era of 'biblical theology' when it was assumed that, with a touch of modernization and with dexterous selection from the biblical material, New Testament theology is immediately relevant to the concerns of the twentieth century, and that its teaching can be applied directly to the problems of modern life.

That era has passed.

Instead we find two different attitudes which are becoming sadly polarized. The first is a return to fundamentalism, often evidenced among those who are influenced by the Charismatic Revival. Such people tend to see the Bible as infallibly written, inspired by God and immediately relevant to the affairs of today. This school of thought fails to take seriously the views and the reasoning of biblical critics, and indeed appears intentionally to remain ignorant of their findings. Difficulties experienced in reconciling different views found within the Bible (or even within the writings of one biblical author) tend to be ignored. These modern fundamentalists do not usually avail themselves of the allegorical method of interpretation by which the ancient authors managed to extricate themselves from these problems. And for the most part they sit light to problems caused by the scientific understanding of the world. Did Paul write that death was due to sin? Then Paul must be right, whatever scientists may say about the inevitability of the ageing process. Does Paul write that there is spiritual wickedness in high places? Then it must be the case that the course of this world is influenced by demonic powers. Did Paul expect the Last Day imminently? Then Paul must be right, whatever cosmologists say about the Second Law of Thermodynamics and the heat death of the planet when the Sun swells up into a Black Giant. Since belief in the Bible's infallibility is to these people a basic dogma, no amount of reasoning is likely to shake their convictions.[2]

It was Rudolf Bultmann, that doyen of New Testament scholarship, who noticed, during the last Great War, that biblical concepts meant nothing or little to the serving soldiers, and he began a stimulating if somewhat academic discussion on his return when he wrote a short article on the need for 'demythologizing' the New Testament.[3] By this he meant that the presuppositions of New Testament times are so different from our own, that a new 'myth' (that is, a framework of images and ideas through which truth is expressed) is needed for a new age. His view was different from that of the 'liberals' who want to bring the Gospel up to date. It required a far more radical approach. However, as Bultmann himself was an Existentialist, following Heidegger's philosophical convictions, his own 'demythologizing' of the Gospel resulted in reducing it to moments of decision when the preacher challenged his hearers with the Word of God. The movement which he started tended to be obscured by his own 'remythologization', which resulted in a Gospel so bare and so reduced as to be scarcely credible to pragmatic Englishmen who did not put as much emphasis on the sermon as is customary in German Lutheran circles. Bultmann's viewpoint led him to give very little importance to the historicity of the gospels, and his prestige as a New Testament scholar initiated a movement which regards the historical element in the gospel material as minimal. All this has led to a school of thought, directly opposed to the Fundamentalist school, which has great reservations about the use of the biblical material as it stands today. The Bible was written, its adherents say, for a different age and a different culture, and today's assumptions are so different from those in the Bible that it is not possible fully to know what the biblical authors really meant when they wrote what they did. The most articulate spokesman for this viewpoint has been Professor Dennis Nincham. He began his Edward Cadbury Lectures in Birmingham with these words:

> One of the main convictions underlying the lectures which follow may be expressed like this: people of different periods and cultures differ very widely: in some cases so widely that accounts of the nature and relations of God, men and the world put forward in one culture may be unacceptable, as they stand, in a different culture, even though they may have expressed profound truth in their time and expressed

it in a form entirely appropriate to the original situation.[4]

In a subsequent lecture in the University of London Profesor Nineham spelled this out a little further:

> For all their good intentions, Christian interpreters of the New Testament, because they believe themselves to be faced with a twofold task, have tried to face all ways, have faltered between two opinions. They have been aware of the peril of modernizing Jesus and the early Church, yet they have been loath to search them out in their full particularity and pastness for fear that in that form they would not speak directly to our condition. Thus they have interpreted New Testament accounts of the past as though they had been written by men who shared our attitude to the past; they have attributed to Jesus that essentially modern hybrid 'realized eschatology'; they have read New Testament teaching on sacrifice, the wrath of God and the rest as if they had been produced by men who shared our understanding of the Old Testament, the nature and demands of God and much else beside.[5]

Nineham concluded his Birmingham lectures with these words:

> As the water of Christian faith has flowed through the various stretches of this river, it has indeed in some respects got clearer and stronger, and it is still the water of life. But from the upper reaches it has also received elements which make it, as it reaches us, *eau non potable* until we have added to it, and killed things in it, as only our generation knows how to do. Our fathers had different palates and other stomachs. Only after appropriate treatment can the water of any

river be health-giving and thirst-quenching to our generation.[6]

Against this background we come to consider Paul for today. Here I must confess that I do not come without presuppositions. In the first place I am not so dismissive of the general claims of the gospels to historical accuracy as others seem to be. So far as Paul is concerned, it is not the whole ministry of Jesus, but only the reality of his death and resurrection which are crucial. Here I take my stand with Bishop Michael Ramsey:

> For my part I find no reason to abandon the traditional view that the body was raised from the tomb, believing it to be congruous with the historical evidence, the understanding of the resurrection in the New Testament generally, and a rational view of divine revelation.[7]

Secondly, there is no need to start all over again the process of Christian thought. I have written elsewhere:

> The evidence forces me to give a very high authority indeed to the contents of the New Testament, not only as a result of critical study, but also because its words so often speak to my whole self – at the deep levels of will and feelings and imagination as well as at the ratiocinative and discursive levels of mind. When read or heard in a discriminating way passages from the Bible (including the Old as well as the New Testament) can not only illumine my path but also become for me, as for others, a vehicle of the Holy Spirit. Yet the Bible does not claim that it is inerrant. Moreover I would expect that within a broad spectrum of theological agreement there exists some theological pluralism; and that is what I find even in the New Testament. I cannot suppose that its

contents will be free from cultural relativism, so that I may expect to 'translate' or 'remythologize' its thought forms and imagery in order to reformulate for myself the truths which the sacred writers were trying to express when they wrote as they did.[8]

This passage was however preceded by an earlier paragraph:

A man's faith is not simply his own. I have received mine through others, and it has been nurtured within the fellowship of the Church. It is intrinsically improbable that the truth about the Christian faith (or of a particular doctrine of the Christian faith) has been hidden down the centuries but has been only lately revealed to me.[9]

It will be clear therefore that in approaching the meaning of Paul for today, I do not come – and no one comes – without presuppositions. For example, I believe that we do know what Paul meant when he wrote on sacrifice, the wrath of God and the like. It is true that we do not share the same attitudes as he did, because our life and thinking is influenced by a very different world outlook. It may be that in our day we shall have to put things differently, and even deny some things that were asserted in the apostolic age, and assert some things which were not thought true in those days. But always underlying what they said there was some truth which must still find expression today, even though our expression of it may take the form of statements to which the early Church could not have agreed, because they did not share our present day assumptions. We should gladly accept the new insights into truth given to this generation through the natural and the human sciences. Is it possible to combine both loyalty to truth as it is now with loyalty to the main inheritance of the Christian faith down the ages?

In order to answer this vital question, it is necessary to clarify the main differences in the assumptions which lie behind the thinking of our age, compared with that of Paul. Perhaps the following are the most important.

1. *Causation.* Paul lived in a world where the connection between cause and effect was very imperfectly understood. Life was full of the unexpected. It was largely unpredictable. God might be subject to the moral laws of his own being; but so far as physical happenings were concerned, he was sovereign. He could do what he willed. He was believed to act directly in human affairs, and not indirectly through primary causes. By contrast we in our age believe in a God who, apart from most exceptional circumstances, limits himself by the regularities of his own creation.

2. *Evolution.* Although there may be discussion today about the *mode* of evolution, both of species and of human culture, there is little doubt about the *fact* of evolution. By contrast, the Jewish world of Paul's day believed in an apocalyptic denouement to this present world age, which God would bring about at his appointed time. Although there was uncertainty about *when* this would be (and Paul himself seems to have changed his ideas on this subject) there was little doubt *that* it would happen. Today the power of mankind to end the present epoch of human beings, through nuclear catastrophe, inclines people to more apocalyptic ways of thinking; but if there were an apocalyptic end to human history as we know it, this would be brought about by man's folly and wickedness, not by God's wrath; and after it had taken place the evolutionary process would begin again.

3. *Scientific knowledge.* Today our knowledge about the universe's origins and development, and the present pattern and structure of the cosmos and all its

constituent parts, animate and inanimate, is due in large measure to the phenomenal success of the scientific method. Although this body of knowledge is always liable to be refined through new knowledge and the success of new scientific hypotheses, and we are now learning to discard mechanical models to illuminate life processes, our assumptions about the world are very different from those of pre-scientific days.

4. *Three-decker universe.* In Paul's day, heaven was believed to be above the sky, and hell beneath our feet. Although it is hard to eliminate the idea of height from any expression of divine transcendence, this is recognized today to be metaphorical. For God is without body or parts, and the localization of heaven and hell is a concession to the limitations of human thought and speech, rather than a literal description of reality.

5. *Human Beings.* Although there is (and always will be) a certain mystery about a human being, because of his openness to the spiritual reality that transcends him, at the same time a very great deal is now known about personal being, and about the social behaviour of individuals and groups. While there is today no generally accepted psychological or sociological theory which can explain man's thinking and willing and feeling, many penetrating insights into the human condition which were completely unknown in biblical times are generally accepted today.

6. *Attitude to Old Testament.* In addition to these general differences between our times and Paul's age, there are further differences due to Paul's Jewish background. For example, he took for granted, in a way which we cannot, the verbal inspiration of the Old Testament, and the goodness and holiness of the Jewish law. Although no Christian today would be likely to side with people like Marcion[10] who disapproved wholly of the Old Testament, most would be discriminating in the approval which they might wish to give it.

How does Paul's thinking appear today if these different assumptions are borne in mind? Our views towards sin, death, and the law are likely to be different from his. For example, Paul believed, on the basis of Genesis 3:19, that death was the result of sin. We now know that it is the inevitable outcome of a built-in ageing process in the human body. Moreover, the ecology of the planet is bound up with predation, and with the use of nutrients from dead bodies, to fertilize the soil for fresh life. Death, far from being a disaster, is a *sine qua non* for new life. It is built into the structure of life, so that it is not possible to conceive of life on this planet without death. As for sin, Paul sees it in many aspects, sometimes as an act of disobedience, partly as a kind of contagion which infests human life, and partly as the result of the baneful influence of evil powers. He believed that sin spread to the whole human race because of Adam's act of disobedience, which constituted the primal sin. It is unacceptable to us today to believe that sin was or is caused directly by the Devil, or by demonic powers. Nor can we now believe that there was a primal sin. Just as it is not possible, during the process of adolescence, to isolate a moment when a person sins for the first time, so also when men emerged from their animal ancestors during the process of evolution, no particular point for a primal sin can be isolated in time. And even if it could be, it would not be possible to imagine that this sin passed to the entire human race by heredity. This would be a particularly flagrant case of the inheritance of acquired characteristics!

Although Paul's thought on death and sin cannot be endorsed today, none the less, in the language and thought forms of his time, he is drawing attention to matters of quite fundamental importance. Death *may* be due to sin, and even when it is not, there is a feeling of 'wrongness' about it, because life is precious. And while we cannot know for certain the cause of human sin, we are all involved in the solidarity of sin. It is universally prevalent, both among religious and irreligious. It is to be found within the Covenant as much as outside it. But modern man cannot accept that it leads to *total* spiritual death, as Paul at times seems to represent it. Sin is always serious, because disobedience to God is serious, and alienation from God means frustration and incompleteness. Most people are a mixture of good and bad, and while no human being has cause for self-justification, most people's lives are not *totally* displeasing to God.

Paul's views about the Jewish Law are partly due to his personal scrupulosity and partly due to his certitude that God called Gentiles into the Church without requiring them to submit to the Jewish Law.[11] For this reason perhaps he exaggerates the ill effects of legal observance. While it is certainly true both that to obey any set of rules is likely to engender a feeling of pride and self-satisfaction, and that most rules are contra-suggestive, evil results are not inevitable. For example, Psalm 119 is a meditation on keeping the Jewish Law, and while undoubtedly it contains passages which are purely moralistic, it would be hard to claim that the Psalm as a whole breathes a complacent air of merit earned through good works, or that observance of the Law led its composers to feel dissatisfaction. Paul himself seems to follow the Jewish Law (if the story of his arrest be regarded as historical), and he himself is not averse to laying down laws of Christian behaviour to his Christian congregations. None the less there is a great truth underlying Paul's attack on the effects of the Jewish Law. Gospel is quite different from Law. The good news of Christ is not that we have managed to attain a prescribed standard of behaviour, but that God has deigned to take us to himself, just as we are. In the peculiar circumstances in which Paul lived, this inevitably showed itself in his teaching as an attack on those who believed that the only way to God was through the keeping of the Jewish Law.

We have seen the great truths for our time which underlie Paul's teaching on sin, death and law. What he writes about 'living after the flesh' is of immediate relevance to the materialism all too evident in the developed world today. To live enclosed within the boundaries of one's own personal self-satisfaction, instead of being open to the needs of others and to the demands of God, is indeed spiritual death. Such an attitude leads to covetousness, pride and sensual gratification. Today Paul's critique may seem to some a little naïve, for we now know that the paths into this sad and tragic situation may be many and varied, and in the modern world there exist many palliatives (such as medication) and anodynes (such as addiction to alcohol, drugs or tobacco) by which people may try consciously or unconsciously to drown their awareness of this tragic condition in which they find themselves. None the less Paul's description of what it means to 'live after the flesh' rings horribly true in the modern world.

Paul sees relief through, and only through, the work of Jesus Christ. In his particular context it was impossible for Paul to know the other great world faiths, such as Buddhism, Hinduism and Mohammedanism at their best. Some of them did not then even exist. He could not know the hidden Christ within them. Paul only had acquaintance with the gnostic beliefs and the mystery religions of the Mediterranean world, together with philosophical systems such as Stoicism. Perhaps his own experience and his own situation blinded him to the best in Judaism: at any rate he attacked the Law in a way quite foreign to Jesus, who is reported to have opposed not the Law itself, but the traditions of the Law as taught by certain Pharisees. Paul lampooned Rabbinic Judaism, so strong were his feelings. But here again there is a fundamental truth underlying Paul's teaching.

It concerns the uniqueness of Christ. Paul knew that Jesus uniquely disclosed God, and uniquely accomplished his work. There could be no substitute for what God had done through him.

What are we to make today of Paul's conception of the person of Jesus himself? He thought of him as a pre-existent being. It is true that there is a certain amount of evidence (which falls far short of demonstration) for re-incarnation;[12] but Paul believed that Jesus was a pre-existent *heavenly* being before he was incarnate on earth. The intellectual climate in which we live today makes such an assumption almost impossible. Paul evidently believed in the full humanity of Jesus, and our knowledge of genetics makes it difficult for us to share the views of the ancient world about the possibility of combining heavenly pre-existence with a human genetical inheritance. But here again there is a fundamental truth underlying Paul's belief. He was concerned to assert the divinity as well as the humanity of Jesus.

He called him God's Son. In so far as he refers to a pre-existent 'metaphysical' person who co-existed with the Father, such thought-forms are alien to contemporary ways of thinking. But in so far as a son bears the character and inheritance of his father and (in a male-dominated culture) is the person who is in the closest personal relationship with him, the appellation is still apt. Perhaps today we should not have the same hesitation that Paul seems to have felt in speaking about God as incarnate in Jesus; and we do not feel the need of the Son's mediation in creation. There are times however when Paul here uses language which seems to speak direct to our present condition, when (for example) he speaks of Jesus as one 'in whom all the fullness of God dwelt in human personality' (*somatikos*). Again, Paul's conviction that God's self-disclosure in this unique personal way showed his humility and love for mankind reaches across the centuries and finds an echo in human hearts today.

Paul called Jesus 'Christ' and 'Lord'. For him Christ was almost a proper name; but there were times when it had overtones of the Messiah. While this is meaningful today to one who (like myself) values his Jewish inheritance, it must be admitted that the fact that Jesus fulfilled the true aspirations of Judaism means little to the predominantly Gentile Church of today. For most people to call Jesus the Messiah is the result of knowing him as Lord, rather than a cause for so doing. 'Lord' implies an object of adoration and worship; and as such it is as relevant to us as it was to Paul.

But, we may ask, is it mere pietism today to speak of *knowing* Christ as Lord? Is this a mere exercise in fantasy to imagine that as a believer I am in a truly personal relationship with Christ, and so to address him as my Lord? Here perhaps we may distinguish between a two-sidedly personal relationship and a one-sidedly personal relationship. Since Christ expresses and embodies for us God in human terms, our human experience of God can be expressed as experience of Christ; but since God is not a person – it would be more accurate to say that there is a personality in God[13] – and since God is not subject to the limitations inherent in being a person, then we can and do react to him as to a person, but he does not in turn address us as person to person. However much we may cut God down to size by thinking of him in personal terms, he addresses us as one who is transcendent over us as well as active within us.

Paul was clear that Jesus has the function of God, even if he could not equate him with God – and here again his words reach across the divide of the centuries. More important for Paul however than who Christ is, is what he does. He speaks of Christ's work in terms of sacrifice, atonement, reconciliation, justification and redemption.

We have already noted that the doctrine of justification through Christ is central to Paul's religious convictions. Does this concept need to be 'demythologized' for today? Certainly it needs to be removed from its context of the Jewish Law, as this is no longer relevant for all but a tiny minority of the world today. It needs to be placed in the larger context of modern anxieties. Paul Tillich wrote:

In the centre of the Protestant courage of confidence stands the courage to accept acceptance in spite of the consciousness of guilt . . . One could say that the courage to be is the courage to accept oneself as accepted in spite of being unacceptable. One does not need to remind the theologians of the fact that this is the genuine meaning of the Paulinian-Lutheran doctrine of 'justification by faith' (a doctrine which in its original phrasing has become incomprehensible even for students of theology). But one must remind theologians and ministers that in the fight against the anxiety of guilt by psychotherapy, the idea of acceptance has received the attention and gained the significance which in the Reformation period was to be seen in phrases like 'forgiveness of sin' or 'justification through faith'. Accepting acceptance though being unacceptable is the basis for the courage of confidence.

Decisive for this affirmation is its being independent of any moral, intellectual or religious precondition: it is not the good or the wise or the pious who are entitled to the courage to accept acceptance, but those who are lacking in all these qualities and are aware of being unacceptable. This however does not mean acceptance by oneself as oneself . . . It is the paradoxical act in which one is accepted by that which infinitely transcends one's individual self . . . Religion asks for the ultimate source of the power which heals by accepting the unacceptable: it asks for God.[14]

Tillich realized that the modern world needs not only justification through faith from guilt, but also from meaninglessness and fear. The world of Paul (and for that matter the world of the Reformers) seems to many today to be pre-occupied with guilt. Deeper self-awareness, and perhaps the changing attitudes which belong to a different culture, combine to shift the emphasis today from guilt to fear and *Angst*. Here perhaps at first sight there seems to loom up a great chasm between our world and that of Paul. Paul believed that our good conduct did not earn merit from God. All, he believed, comes from God's grace. He takes no pride in himself, but he boasts only in Christ. 'I count everything sheer loss, because all is far outweighed by the gain of knowing Christ Jesus my Lord, for whose sake I did in fact lose everything. I count it so much garbage, for the sake of gaining Christ and finding myself incorporate in him, with no righteousness of my own, no legal rectitude, but the righteousness that comes from faith in Christ' (Philippians 3:8f). This kind of self-sacrifice hardly seems consistent with the concept of self-affirmation, which lies at the root of modern thinking about freedom from fear and *Angst*. Certainly Paul's thought here needs elaboration in the light of modern knowledge, but not denial. We have come to realize the fundamental truth that before we have a self which we can freely offer to God as a sacrifice, we must first affirm ourselves.

But is the concept of sacrifice still viable today? There is only a folk memory of its true meaning, derived from war memorials to those 'who laid down their lives' during the last two Great Wars. For most people the idea of sacrifice does not lead naturally to the Cross (as it did in Paul's day) but vice versa.

By contrast the imagery of redemption or liberation is predominant in popular thought today. Its meaning is often blurred and emotive; but it is an image to which most people immediately respond. No doubt this is because people easily feel alienated from themselves, from their work and from their fellow men; and the end of the colonial era, and the struggle for freedom from economic imperialism (to say nothing of the women's movement) adds to the popular desire for freedom. Liberation Theology stems from the basic concept of freedom. No doubt there is a danger here, into which in the first flush of enthusiasm many liberation theologians seem to have fallen, of reducing the Gospel to a social and political quasi-Marxist programme, instead of concentrating on the liberation that Christ brought to the world.[15] Today people no longer want to speak in Pauline phrases about redemption; but in so far as redemption leads to freedom this is still a key concept in speaking of the work of Christ. Perhaps many would prefer today most of all an image which Paul himself seldom uses in his extant writings; the personal image of reconciliation. Once again this is a popular concept today, with industrial reconciliation services, and with many estranged groups and couples within modern society. We can also give an extended meaning to Christ the Reconciler, different from that of Paul's day. The existence of universal evil and pain and suffering is more evident to all, perhaps as a result of the mass media, and the question that Job raised about evil and suffering comes to the fore. How can this world be reconciled with a loving Creator? To quote what I have written on this subject elsewhere:

So far as I understand it, the essence of the total biblical picture is that God, through the event of Christ, came to the help of mankind. He did not merely manifest himself: his self-disclosure was a costly act which potentially gives life to all mankind. It was a humble, compassionate, loving act whereby God not only assumed complete humanity, but also suffered the worst that men can do. 'He became sin for us.' 'He became a curse for us.' The writers of the New Testament would not have dared to accuse God of injustice and indifference to the human situation. 'Who are you, O man, to answer back to God? Will what is moulded say to its moulder, "Why have you made me thus?"' asks Paul. But Paul's very horror of such blasphemy suggests that unconsciously he was asking this very question. The Atonement as the answer to man's Great Accusation belongs to the twentieth century; but this thought is not so far removed as it might seem from the unconscious thought and fears of the first century.[16]

The death of Jesus shows us God suffering the worst that his creation can do to him. 'What is salvation? Only if disaster, forsakenness by God, absolute death, the infinite curse of damnation, and sinking into nothingness is in God himself, is community with this God eternal salvation, infinite joy, indestructible election and divine life. The "bifurcation" in God must contain the whole uproar of history within itself. Men must be able to recognize rejection, the curse and final nothingness in it.'[17] That is God's way of reconciliation with man in the midst of the paradoxes of life. 'God in Auschwitz and Auschwitz in the crucified God – that is the basis for a real hope.'[18] This is the context in which a Christian lives 'in Christ'. This is the atmosphere that he breathes in his Christian life.

We may perhaps look finally at three other aspects of Paul's thinking; his doctrine of the Spirit, his view of the Church, and his beliefs about the Last Things.

So far as the Spirit is concerned, Paul has no fully worked out system of belief. The Spirit is the mode through which Christians relate to God in Christ. In the Spirit Christians are related to one another through their common participation in Christ. What are we to make of such language and such thought today? Certainly we are aware of belonging together in the solidarities of existence. It does not really matter whether or not this solidarity is an ontological reality, or whether it is a unity on the level of unconscious and conscious experience. It is possible to identify (and to be identified) with that to which one is not metaphysically united. The consciousness of being identified with Christ brings also an awareness of being united with others who are similarly identified. The Spirit is a way of describing the quality of our conscious awareness of Christ and of Christ's influence on our subconscious selves. Because there is personality in God, and the Spirit is God immanent, we can speak of 'Him'. Because Christ brings out in us our latent potentialities and gifts, we speak of the gifts of the Spirit. Because Christ affects us in our emotional and volitional selves as much (or probably more than) in our reasoning, the Spirit brings us 'religious experience' and warms our relationship with God and with one another. We share in the one Spirit because we are incorporated into an ongoing stream of Christian life. We are not mere individuals, since sharing lies at the very centre of the Christian life. As we learn to open ourselves at deeper and deeper levels to this Christian solidarity, we respond to the immanent God, so that the Spirit helps us to pray when we do not know what to say. There are times when the corporate unconscious may overwhelm us, as when we pray 'in tongues'. But this experience should always be subservient to the main work of the Spirit, which is to build up the Christian solidarity of believers in the power and presence of God in greater maturity.

It seems then that Paul's doctrine of the Spirit may be remythologized into concepts and imageries which have the ring of truth for the twentieth century. None the less, many today would wish to enlarge the New Testament (and therefore the Pauline) concept of the Spirit, so that lines may not be drawn too rigidly between Christians and non-Christians. The Spirit is at work within the cosmos, shaping its ends; and the Spirit binds humanity together. This is not a different Spirit from the Spirit of Christ; for the Spirit in man is the Spirit of the immanent God, and Christ is his personal self-expression, and therefore they are fundamentally united, even if experienced under different aspects.

According to Pauline thought, the Spirit finds its locus within the Christian Church. Today many would not wish to define the edges of the Church as rigidly as Paul does. Baptism admits to the Church, but is there not a baptism of desire? If we think of the People of God, it is a concept that is blurred at the edges, for God wants all to be his People. The images of the bride, the building and the body all contain fundamental truth. All have their uses today as metaphors and analogies – but all of them can be misleading. The doctrine of the Body is a subpersonal analogy which seems to suggest that the various 'members' are parts of an interdependent organism rather than people of infinite worth in their own right. The image of the Bride is used by Paul within the limited understanding of marriage as Paul knew it. For him the bridegroom should love his wife, but the bride has only to obey her husband. Paul uses the concept of marriage to convey an idea of indissolubility between Christ and his Church which many would no longer think of as inevitably constituted by the marriage bond. And a building again suffers to an even greater extent being an impersonal image. These however are minor criticisms of Paul's ecclesiology.

The main question is whether the Church is simply an agglomeration of Christian disciples, or whether we find acceptable Paul's concept of Christians belonging together because they are called and brought together by God. Do Christians constitute the Church, like any other association of people, or are individuals called into an already existing Divine Society? Is the Church merely a sociological phenomenon, subject to all the laws of such associations, or has it, in addition to its institutional aspects, a divine nature which enables it to be renewed after stagnation and decline in a way that no other human society can achieve? The questions raised in this form are answered today differently by different people. But the very fact that this happens shows that the essence of Paul's view of the Church is not alien to twentieth-century assumptions: rather, it is a matter for debate.

Paul's eschatology shows more clearly perhaps than any other aspect of this thought the great divide between first and twentieth centuries. Life will not suddenly end upon the planet. It will die out, as the planet warms up, when, in a million million years' time, the sun begins its death agony. As for individuals,[19] Paul's doctrine of the resurrection of the body seems in some ways curiously modern. The old body decays in the earth (or today it is more likely to be burnt). Out of this there arises a spiritual body, and there will be new relationships of existence in the world of spirit bodies. We enter here a field of speculation; and as we have seen, Paul is not himself always consistent about the Last Things. Until recently many would have doubted whether Paul was right to think of the dead sleeping until the Last Day, when all would rise together to a new life in Christ under new and unimaginable conditions of existence. It was more acceptable to modern thinking to assume that (if there be a resurrection) there is an immediate entry into a spirit world with an opportunity for fresh development so that people may become sufficiently mature to attain the goal of life with God for ever. The modern theory of relativity however, together with the quantum theory, shows how distorted is the idea of the material world which we gain from our senses, and how misleading is our experience of time as duration; and Paul's thinking may be more acceptable to modern scientific assumptions than is popularly thought. While many would question the precision with which Paul speaks of mysteries beyond our understanding, once again the fundamental truths behind what Paul writes need to be emphasized. The judgement and the promise of God are two such truths. There is the promise of progress towards God's final goal for this great experiment of evolution which he has begun and which his Spirit guides and inspires. There is also the realization that progress will not necessarily be even and gradual, but full of hiccups and regressions. And there is also the note of judgement, because painful self-awareness is necessary to spiritual progress, and guilt, fear and anxiety need to be acknowledged before they can be subsumed into a heightened maturity.

In a brief survey such as this, it is only possible to deal with a few selected topics of Paul's theological thinking, and to examine them in the light of contemporary assumptions. It is not possible for an intelligent twentieth-century person to affirm Pauline theology *in toto*, as compatible with the assumptions of modern knowledge and culture. However, the main points of his thinking can be 'remythologized' to form part of the belief system of an intelligent worshipping Christian today, who is anxious to be faithful to the ongoing tradition of the Church and to be an honest man of his own time. The basic themes of Paul span the different cultures across the centuries.

It seems that in the apostolic age there are present themes concerning the Christian life which are rooted in history and are so characteristically Christian that their recurrence through the subsequent centuries is not surprising. While Christian spirituality has shown a vast range of emphasis and diffusion, times of renewal and recovery have been times of conscious return to one or other of the primitive scriptural themes. Thus St Francis and his followers were inspired by a realization of the cross as well as certain aspects of the earthly life of Jesus. The Reformers had recourse to the Pauline teaching on justification. The Methodist revival was alive with a variety of biblical themes and images. The Tractarians were moved by the Incarnation and the life of the Word made flesh. In every case there is emphasis upon the priority of God's grace to the human response to that grace.[20]

Is it too much to think a return to the Scriptures, and in particular to Paul the Apostle, could bring us another such time of renewal and recovery today?

NOTES

CHAPTER ONE

1   There is no evidence that Peter was big. The phrase is derived from the book of that name, *The Big Fisherman*, by Lloyd C. Douglas. For more scholarly studies see O. Cullmann, *Peter* (SCM Press, London, 1953), and J. Lowe, *Saint Peter* (Oxford University Press, 1956).

2   The phrase was first used by Clement Alex: (*cit.* Eusebius, E. H. 6.14).

3   I have borrowed freely from C. H. Dodd '*The Mind of Paul*' (1933) in *New Testament Studies* (Manchester University Press, 1953), now available as a Fount Paperback. For other useful studies cf. C. A. Anderson Scott, *Saint Paul: The Man and Teacher* (Cambridge University Press, 1936); M. Dibelius, *Paul* (Longmans, London, 1953); G. Bornkamm, *Paul* (Hodder & Stoughton, London, 1971); D. S. Stewart, *A Man in Christ* (Hodder & Stoughton, London, 1935); A. D. Nock, *St Paul* (Oxford University Press, 1946).

4   Of course Luke's authorship of Acts is disputed. For the argument for and against, cf. *The Beginnings of Christianity*, ed. F. Jackson and K. Lake (Macmillan, London, 1922), Part 1, Vol. 2, pp. 207–362.

5   Commonly observed, e.g., in J. Lowe, *op. cit.*, p. 16.

6   Cf. B. S. Easton, 'The Purpose of Acts', *Early Christianity* (SPCK, London, 1955), Part 2.

7   Cf. R. B. Rackham, *The Acts of the Apostles* (Methuen, London, 1904), p. xxxviii.

8   'It is through him that everyone who has faith is acquitted of everything for which there is no acquittal under the law of Moses' (Acts 13:39).

9   Cf. H. J. Cadbury, *The Peril of Modernizing Jesus* (SPCK, London, 1962).

10 For discussion about the nature and course of the Collection, cf. K. F. Nickle, *The Collection* (SCM Press, London, 1966); J. C. Hurd, *The Origin of 1 Corinthians* (SPCK, London, 1965).

11 *Acts of Paul and Thecla*, 3.

12 Cf. L. Finkelstein, *The Pharisees* (The Jewish Publication Society of America, Philadelphia, 1946), Vol. 1, p. 39, who gives an interesting list of examples to prove his point.

13 Rabbi Gamaliel I was Rabbi Hillel's grandson. Doubt has been

expressed that anyone who had studied under Gamaliel could have had such a distorted view of Jewish Law.

14 Cf. Sir William Ramsay, *St Paul the Traveller and Roman Citizen* (Hodder & Stoughton, London, 1896), p. 130.

15 Cf. C. G. Montefiore, *Judaism and St Paul* (Goschem, London, 1914), who believed Paul was not a Rabbinic but a Hellenistic Jew. H. J. Schoeps (*Paul*, Lutterworth, London, 1961, pp.47ff), also writing from a Jewish point of view, sees Paul with a mixture of Hellenistic and Rabbinic Judaism. W. D. Davies, however, (*Paul and Rabbinic Judaism*, SPCK, London, 1948, p. vii) reads him against a Rabbinic background. E. P. Sanders (*Paul and Palestinian Judaism*, SCM Press, London, 1977) holds that Paul misrepresented Rabbinic attitudes to Law, which are best described as 'covenantal nomism'. He believes that for Paul 'the solution precedes the problem'.

16 *Op. cit.*, p. 71.

17 W. C. Van Unnik questions whether Paul really came from Tarsus (*Tarsus or Jerusalem*, Epworth, London, 1962). For a description of Tarsus, and the cities visited by Paul, cf. Sir William Ramsey, *The Cities of St Paul* (Hodder & Stoughton, London, 1907).

18 Cf. W. L. Knox, *St Paul and the Church of Gentiles* (Cambridge University Press, 1939).

19 Cf. J. H. Moulton and G. Milligan, *The Vocabulary of the Greek Testament* (Hodder & Stoughton, London, 1930); W. F. Arndt and F. W. Gingrich, *A Greek-English Lexicon of the New Testament* (Cambridge University Press, 1957).

20 Cf. A. Deissmann, *Light From the Ancient East* (Hodder & Stoughton, London, 1910), pp. 323ff.

21 For the population of the Diaspora, cf. C. Guignebert, *The Jewish World in the Time of Jesus* (Routledge & Kegan Paul, London, 1939) p. 215. Philo tells us that there were one million Jews in Alexandria alone, and Guignebert thinks that there may have been a total of seven million in the Diaspora, probably including proselytes.

22 For the population of Palestine, cf. J. Jeremias, *Jerusalem in the Time of Jesus* (SCM Press, London, 1967) p. 205.

23 For a sensitive exposition of the universalist case, cf. J. A. T. Robinson, *In the End God* (James Clarke, London, 1950), Chapter 9.

24 Cf. J. Munck, *Paul and the Salvation of Mankind* (SCM Press, London, 1959).

25 See note 10.

26 Cf. Hugh Montefiore, 'Jesus and the Temple Tax' in *New Testament Studies*, 10, pp. 60–71. Large movements of money

from the Jews of the Dispersion could cause great problems in the bullion market! (cf. Cicero, *Pro Flacco*, 28.)

27 *Op. cit.*, pp. 71f.

28 Cf. A. Deissmann, *Paul* (Hodder & Stoughton, London, 1926), p. 6.

29 Cf. A. Schweitzer, *The Mysticism of Paul the Apostle* (A. & C. Black, London, 1953).

30 *Op. cit.*, p. 81.

31 See Chapter 3, pp. 57–61, for a fuller account.

32 See Chapter 4, p. 108f, for a fuller exposition of the doctrine.

CHAPTER TWO

1 K. H. Rengstorf, *Apostleship* (A. & C. Black, London, 1952), p. 33.

2 *Op. cit.*, p. 43.

3 For Jewish elders in Hellenistic synagogues cf. article by G. Bornkamm under *Presbys* in Kittel's *Theological Dictionary of the New Testament* (Eerdmans, Grand Rapids, 1968), Vol. 6, pp. 660ff., and A. E. Harvey, 'Elders', *Journal of Theological Studies*, N. S., Vol. 25, Part 2, pp. 318ff.

4 For a distinction made between *episcopi* and presbyters in the New Testament, cf. A. Farrer, 'Ministry in the New Testament', *The Apostolic Ministry*, ed. K. E. Kirk (Hodder & Stoughton, London, 1946), pp. 113ff. For the view that the historic episcopate emerged out of the presbyterate cf. J. B. Lightfoot, Dissertation 1, *Commentary on Philippians* (Macmillan, London, 1885). For a judicious evaluation cf. T. W. Manson, *The Church's Ministry* (Hodder & Stoughton, London, 1948).

5 J. A. T. Robinson, 'Kingdom, Church and Ministry', *The Historic Episcopate*, ed. K. Carey (A. & C. Black, London, 1954), p. 15.

6 Cf. R. R. Williams, *Authority in the Apostolic Age* (SCM Press, London, 1950), p. 47.

7 B. H. Streeter (*The Primitive Church*, Macmillan, London, 1929) examined Harnack's thesis that prophets, like apostles, exercised a universal ministry in the Church, compared with the local ministries of presbyter-bishops and deacons, but preferred to postulate on original diversity, a rapid evolution in response to urgent local needs, to be followed later by standardization (*op. cit.*, p. 72).

8 Cf. R. N. Flew, *Jesus and His Church* (Epworth, London, 1938), where reasons are given for Jesus envisaging a community living

under God's kingly rule, e.g. the ecclesia, but without the institutionalization which has later developed.

9   For a summary of these, cf. C. A. Anderson Scott, *op. cit.*, pp. 13ff.

10   Cf. C. H. Dodd, *The Apostolic Preaching and Its Developments* (Hodder & Stoughton, London, 1936) who holds that they are not fabrications. But see, on the other hand, C. F. Evans, 'The Kerygma', *Journal of Theological Studies*, N. S., Vol. 7, Part 1, pp. 25ff., who comes to a contrary conclusion.

11   But not the most original or forceful in the early Church! In the author's judgement, that attribution should be given to Apollos. Cf. Hugh Montefiore, *The Epistle to the Hebrews* (A. & C. Black, London, 1964), pp. 1–28.

12   For the arguments in favour cf. E. G. Selwyn, *The First Epistle of St Peter* (Macmillan, Lonlon, 1946), pp. 7–36; and for the other side, F. W. Beare, *The First Epistle of Peter* (Blackwell, Oxford, 1958), pp. 1–31. F. L. Cross, *1 Peter: A Paschal Liturgy* (Mowbrays, London, 1954), believed that it was a liturgical document.

13   Hugh Montefiore, *op. cit, supra.*

14   C. H. Dodd, *op. cit.*, p. 16.

15   Although there are not lacking scholars who date Acts late and deny Lucan authorship, there is impressive testimony in favour. W. L. Knox (*The Acts of the Apostles*, Cambridge University Press, 1948, p. 65), assessing the Acts' reliability as a historical document, writes: 'Within its limits it appears to be high but we must remember its limits.' M. Hengel (*Acts and the History of Earliest Christianity*, SCM Press, London, 1979, p. 38) writes: 'For all his tendentious distortions, Luke's contribution to the historical understanding of Paul is essentially greater than many scholars want to suppose today.' The classical historian A. N. Sherwin-White (*Roman Society and Roman Law in the New Testament*, Oxford University Press, 1963, p. 189) declares: 'For Acts the confirmation of historicity is overwhelming.'

16   Cf. H. B. Mattingly, 'On the Origin of the Name Christianoi', *Journal of Theological Studies*, N. S., Vol. 9, Part 1, pp. 26ff.

17   The alternative, that these passages were specially fabricated to lend verisimilitude to Acts, is hardly a credible hypothesis.

18   *E. H.*, 3.5.

19   Cf. *New Testament Apocrypha*, ed. R. McR. Wilson (Lutterworth, London, 1963), Vol. 1, pp. 158ff.

20   S. G. F. Brandon, *The Fall of Jerusalem and the Christian Church* (SPCK, London, 1951, p. 72), held that Paul was opposed by Jewish Christians because he was a latecomer to the Christian faith who had neither been an eye-witness of Jesus's ministry

Notes

nor knew the original tradition about him. Brandon, assuming that the Synoptic Gospels were written after A.D. 70, sees them as adulterated witness of the primitive Palestinian tradition.

21 Cf. J. A. T. Robinson, *Redating the New Testament* (SCM Press, London, 1979). For the sake of convenience, the dating of the main events of Paul's ministry – about which there is little controversy, apart from J. Knox (*Chapters in a Life of Paul*, A. & C. Black, New York, 1950) – are accepted as given there. E. E. Ellis, in 'Dating the New Testament', *New Testament Studies*, Vol. 26, No. 4, pp. 487–502, adduces additional reasons for adopting Robinson's hypothesis that all books of the New Testament were completed before A.D. 70.

22 J. A. T. Robinson, *op. cit. supra.*

23 E. J. Goodspeed's original theory has been elaborated by John Knox (*Philemon Among the Letters of Paul*).

24 Cf. C. L. Mitton, *The Formation of the Pauline Corpus* (Epworth, London, 1955), for a succinct and judicious survey.

25 C. L. Mitton, *op. cit.*, pp. 75ff.

CHAPTER THREE

1 *The Translator's New Testament* (British and Foreign Bible Society, London, 1973).

2 A. Q. Morton, *Christianity and the Computer* (Hodder & Stoughton, London, 1964), for studies of *Kai* and *de*.

3 Cf. A. Deissmann, *Light From the Ancient East* (Hodder & Stoughton, London, 1910).

4 Cf. C. L. Mitton, *Formation of the Pauline Corpus of Letters* (Epworth, London, 1955, p. 67). The earliest Christian scriptures seem to have been written as *codices*, not rolls.

5 This was not their original order. Marcion in the second century A.D. used the following order: Galatians, 1 and 2 Corinthians, Romans, 1 and 2 Thessalonians, Ephesians, Colossians, Philemon and Philippians (Epiphanius, *Haeres* xiii). It has been suggested that 1 and 2 Corinthians and 1 and 2 Thessalonians formed single epistles, and that Philemon was added to Colossians.

6 For an account of Paul and his thought by means of considering each epistle in turn, L. Grollenberg (*Paul*, SCM Press, London, 1978) could hardly be bettered.

7 For a recent excellent exposition of Romans see J. A. T. Robinson, *Wrestling with Romans* (SCM Press, London, 1979).

Of the many excellent commentaries on the letters of Paul, those in the Black and Moffatt series (and the Clarendon Bible) are on the English text.

8 J. Armitage Robinson, *St Paul's Epistle to the Ephesians* (James Clarke, London n.d., p. 10).

9 J. B. Lightfoot, *The Epistles of St Paul: Colossians and Philemon* (Macmillan, London, 1890, p. 113).

10 *Op. cit.*, p. 114.

CHAPTER FOUR

1 For a history of nineteenth-century interpretation cf. A. Schweitzer, *Paul and His Interpreters* (A. & C. Black, London, 1912), and for a more restricted but more modern survey, cf. E. E. Ellis, *Paul and His Recent Interpreters* (Eerdmans, Grand Rapids, 1961).

2 For surveys of Pauline theology, cf. H. A. A. Kennedy, *Theology of the Epistles* (Duckworth, London, 1923), pp. 28–160. R. Bultmann, *The Theology of the New Testament* (SCM Press, London, 1953), pp. 187–345; D. E. Whiteley, *The Theology* of St Paul (Blackwell, Oxford, 1964).

3 For Paul's anthropology cf. J. A. T. Robinson, *The Body* (SCM Press, London, 1952), pp. 11–48; E. Käsemann, 'On Paul's Anthropology', *Pauline Perspectives* (SCM Press, London, 1971), pp. 1–31; W. D. Stacey, *The Pauline Doctrine of Man* (Macmillan, London, 1956).

4 Cf. C. Ryder Smith, *The Biblical Doctrine of Sin* (Epworth, London, 1953), Part 3.

5 C. H. Dodd (*Moffatt Commentary on the Epistle to the Romans*, Hodder & Stoughton, London, 1932) believed that the Wrath was 'impersonal': 'Sin is the cause: disaster the effect', p. 23. But this is to misunderstand Paul's personal conception of God who can say 'Vengeance is mine: I will repay' (Romans 12:19).

6 Cf. R. S. Shedd, *Man in Community* (Epworth, London, 1958), for a study of human solidarity in Pauline thought.

7 For Paul's Christology, cf. in particular A. E. J. Rawlinson, *The New Testament Doctrine of Christ* (Longmans, London, 1926), pp. 81–166; L. Cerfaux, *Christ in the Theology of St Paul* (Herder & Herder, London, 1959).

8 J. A. T. Robinson's attempt (*The Human Face of God*, SCM Press, London, 1973, pp. 162ff) to prove that Paul did not here refer to the pre-existence is special pleading: a better case to the

contrary is found in R. G. Hamerton-Kelly, *Pre-existence, Wisdom and the Son of Man* (Cambridge University Press, Cambridge, 1973).

9   For studies of sacrifice, cf. S. C. Gayford, *Sacrifice and Priesthood* (London 1924); R. K. Yerkes, *Sacrifice* (A. & C. Black, London, 1953); F. Young, *Sacrifice and the Death of Christ* (SPCK, London, 1975).

10   Cf. A. Deissmann, *Light from the Ancient East* (Hodder & Stoughton, London, 1910) pp. 323ff.

11   Cf. C. H. Dodd, *The Bible and the Greeks* (Hodder & Stoughton, London, 1935) pp. 42–58; V. Taylor, *Forgiveness and Reconciliation* (Macmillan, London, 1952) pp. 29–69.

12   Cf. R. Bultmann, *op. cit.*, pp. 314ff.

13   Cf. P. S. Watson, *The Concept of Grace* (Epworth, London, 1959) pp. 11–17.

14   Cf. J. A. T. Robinson, *The Body*, (SCM Press, London) p. 51. For a less metaphysical interpretation of Paul's thought here, cf. E. Best, *One Body in Christ* (SPCK, London, 1955).

15   For an understanding of the phrase 'in Christ' cf. L. S. Thornton, *Common Life in the Body of Christ* (Dacre, London, 1942); A. R. George, *Communion with God in the New Testament* (Epworth, London, 1953) pp. 140–95.

16   Cf. H. B. Swete, *The Holy Spirit in the New Testament* (Macmillan, London, 1909) pp. 167–253; E. Schweitzer, *The Spirit of God* (A. & C. Black, London 1960) pp. 54–87.

17   Cf. W. F. Flemington, *The New Testament Doctrine of Baptism* (SPCK, London, 1948); O. Cullmann, *Baptism in the New Testament* (SCM Press, London, 1950).

18   For Pauline ethics, cf. C. A. Anderson Scott, *New Testament Ethics* (Cambridge University Press, Cambridge, 1930) pp. 73–130.

19   For an interesting comparison between the ethics of Paul and Seneca, cf. J. N. Sevenster, *Paul and Seneca* (Brill, Leiden, 1961), pp. 167–218.

20   Cf. L. Cerfaux, *The Church in the Theology of St Paul* (Herder & Herder, London, 1959).

21   Cf. O. Cullmann, *The State in the New Testament* (SCM Press, London, 1957) pp. 87f; *Christ and Time* (SCM Press, London, 1951).

22   However, Paul makes it quite clear that the spiritual does not come first (as Philo thought), but the animal body of which the spiritual is raised up (1 Corinthians 15:44).

23   For Pauline eschatology cf. T. F. Glasson, *Second Advent* (Epworth, London, 1945, pp. 207ff); H. A. Guy, *The New Testament Doctrine of the Last Things* (Oxford University Press,

Notes

1948) pp. 102–28; J. A. T. Robinson, *op. cit.*, pp. 49–84.

24 Cf. J. Barr, *The Semantics of Biblical Literature* (Oxford University Press, 1961) pp. 8ff.

CHAPTER FIVE

1 C. H. Dodd, *The Meaning of Paul for Today* (Fount Paperbacks, London, 1958), p. 11.

2 Cf. J. Barr, *Fundamentalism* (SCM Press, London, 1977) for a penetrating if unsympathetic account.

3 Cf. *Kerygma and Myth*, ed. H. W. Bartsch (SPCK, London, 1972).

4 D. E. Nineham, *The Use and Abuse of the Bible* (Macmillan, London, 1976), p. 1.

5 D. E. Nineham, *New Testament Interpretation in a Historical Age* (Athlone, London, 1976), p. 22.

6 Cf. *The Use and Abuse of the Bible*, p. 232.

7 A. M. Ramsey, *Jesus and the Living Past* (Oxford University Press, 1980), p. 31.

8 *Christian Believing* (SPCK, London, 1976), p. 148.

9 ibid.

10 Marcion was the arch heretic of the second-century Church who believed that the God of the Old Testament was not the Father of our Lord Jesus Christ.

11 E. P. Sanders, *op. cit.*, believes that his views on the Law were largely formed as a result of his convictions about Christ. But it was Paul's views about gentile Christians which most affected his attitude to the Jewish Law.

12 E.g. J. Iverson, *More Lives Than One?* (Souvenir Press, London, 1976).

13 Cf. C. C. J. Webb, *God and Personality* (London, 1918).

14 *The Courage To Be* (Nisbet & Co Ltd, London, 1952, and Fount Paperbacks, 1977), p. 156.

15 John Finnis lists 'six conditions which bracket the meaning of liberation in Catholic theology as expounded by the Roman magisterium' ('Catholic Social Teaching', *Church Alert*, No. 19, Geneva, 1978, pp. 6f). Few of these are fulfilled in e.g. G. Guiterrez, *A Theology of Liberation* (SCM Press, London, 1974).

16 Hugh Montefiore, *Awkward Questions on Christian Love* (Fontana, London, 1964), pp. 90f.

17 J. Moltmann, *The Crucified God* (SCM Press, London, 1974), p. 246.

18 J. Moltmann, *op. cit.*, p. 278.
19 For an interpretation of Paul's eschatology in terms not of individuals but of the Church, cf. J. A. T. Robinson, *In the End God*, quoted above.
20 A. M. Ramsey, *op. cit.*, p. 59.

Fount Paperbacks

Fount is one of the leading paperback publishers of religious books and below are some of its recent titles.

- ☐ SQUARE WORDS IN A ROUND WORLD Eric Kemp 95p
- ☐ THE HOLY SPIRIT Billy Graham 95p
- ☐ REACHING OUT Henri Nouwen 95p
- ☐ DEATH & AFTER: WHAT WILL REALLY HAPPEN?
      H. J. Richards £1.25
- ☐ GO AN EXTRA MILE Michael Wood 95p
- ☐ HAPPY FAMILIES Anthony Bullen 95p
- ☐ THE NEW INQUISITION? SCHILLEBEECKX AND KÜNG
      Peter Hebblethwaite £1.25
- ☐ CHRISTIANITY AND OTHER RELIGIONS
      John Hick & Brian Hebblethwaite £1.50
- ☐ TOWARDS THE DAWN Clifford Hill £1.25
- ☐ THE POPE FROM POLAND John Whale £1.50
- ☐ THE FAITH OF AN ANGLICAN Gilbert Wilson £2.95
- ☐ PRAYER FOR PILGRIMS Sheila Cassidy £1.50

All Fount paperbacks are available at your bookshop or news-agent, or they can also be ordered by post from Fount Paperbacks, Cash Sales Department, G.P.O. Box 29, Douglas, Isle of Man, British Isles. Please send purchase price, plus 10p per book. Customers outside the U.K. send purchase price, plus 12p per book. Cheque, postal or money order. No currency.

NAME (Block letters) _____

ADDRESS _____

_____

_____